CW01560798

LEGAL DISCLAIMER

This book is the author's personal interpretation and research of each style and how it is being used currently. It is <u>not</u> a history of Interior Design period styles reference. If that's what you are looking for, find a list of recommended references at the end of the book.

The information provided within this book is for **general informational and educational purposes only**. The author makes no representations or warranties, express or implied, about the completeness, accuracy, reliability, suitability or availability with respect to the information, products, services, or related graphics contained in this book for any purpose. Any use of this information is at your own risk.

Information is written & curated by **Aseel A. H. Ahmad**
Cover Illustration Copyright © 2020 by Aseel A. H. Ahmad
Cover design by Aseel A. H. Ahmad (@aseelbysketchbook)
www.aseelbysketchbook.com
All illustrations © 2020 Aseel A. H. Ahmad

All rights reserved. No parts of the content of this book may be reproduced or distributed in public, without the prior written permission of the author. All images are copyright to their respective owners and are protected under international copyright laws.. Without prior written permission, it is not permitted to copy, download, or reproduce these images in any way whatsoever.

THE INTERIOR DESIGN *Styles* LOOKBOOK

© ASEEL BY SKETCHBOOK 2020 | All Rights Reserved

HOW *Styles* THIS
CAME *lookbook* TO LIFE:

the original
styles lookbook
2013-2014

When I was a 22-year-old looking for a chance at practicing what I just graduated, I got my first interview to work as a junior interior Designer in a cute little company. Needless to say, being the A-Student I was, I made sure to thoroughly research the company before I conducted my interview. I wanted to impress them on the first try. During my research, I found out that they value Interior Design Styles so much that they built a marketplace for their bespoke products according to the Interior Design styles that were popular at the time. To prepare for the interview, I grabbed my bright red Moleskine notebook and created a mini "reference" for myself to remember the styles and what the main characteristics of each style were. I wanted that job so bad, and to my relief, I got that job (to be honest, I don't know if I got it because of the red Moleskine, but I certainly had fun sketching, researching, and learning about styles).

I quit that job 4 months later, but what I gained from that experience was far from ordinary. I got the idea of this book 7 years ago, and it has been in the back of my mind for a while, I even remember that during a "fun day" when I was working in IKEA, we had this ice breaker "speed dating" game where you had to tell the other person what your hopes and dreams are. I didn't even know that this is what I had in mind, it was a 1-minute decision and I said I wanted to write a reference book about interior design styles. I feel quite amused that I haven't started this earlier.

Lots of things have happened since then, I started a YouTube Channel where I showed my now "vintage" Moleskine, and I got a tremendous amount of messages, comments and requests asking me to talk more about the styles in Interior Design. So naturally, when I finally got the chance to start this book, I redid my research, I rolled up my sleeves and got to work. As Steve Jobs once said: "You can't connect the dots looking forward; you can only connect them looking backward. So you have to trust that the dots will somehow connect in your future. You have to trust in something - your gut, destiny, life, karma, whatever. This approach has never let me down, and it has made all the difference in my life."

If you do enjoy this book, then it's because I put my heart and soul into it for more time than I can remember.
Thank you so much for supporting me and buying my project of passion. I hope you get a lot of value out of what I gathered for you. All love to you.

Aseel

contents

contents

الحمد لله

dedication

To the souls of my wonderful parents, may they Rest in Peace. Thank you, **Mom and Dad**, for giving me all the love, support and everything I have ever needed to get to this level, I miss you, I love you, even if you can't see it, I know you are proud. You were, still are, and will always be the best parents in the world.

To my wonderful husband, **Ali**, for providing a supportive and safe environment for me to work on my project of passion. For believing in me, for taking care of me & for being the best support system ever. I love you, I adore you, I cherish you, I am so grateful to have you. Always & forever. I couldn't have done it without you.

To my sisters, **Einas & Ghaida**, I can't tell you how grateful I am to have 2 incredible sisters by my side, thank you for encouraging me, thank you for supporting me, I am so lucky to have the both of you, thank you for being my cheerleaders and my critics at the same time. I love you so much.

To my siblings and nieces and nephews (especially my nephew, **Omar**) thank you for believing in me and pushing me with your kindness and your words of encouragement. I love you.

To my friends who made me laugh and gave me space when I needed to work, for their support, for their kindness, for their words of wisdom. I love you.

Thank you, **Lina**, for being my rock through a lot of things, and for supporting me unconditionally

Thank you my kindest **Amna & Aisha Al Nuaimi** for giving me so much support through the thick and thin. I love you, I am so grateful to have you.

Each person I have met, in real life or the internet, I am thankful for **YOU!** You have 100% touched my life in more ways than you can imagine, thank you for your support, and thank you for buying this book! I hope you find value in my work.

with all of my love,

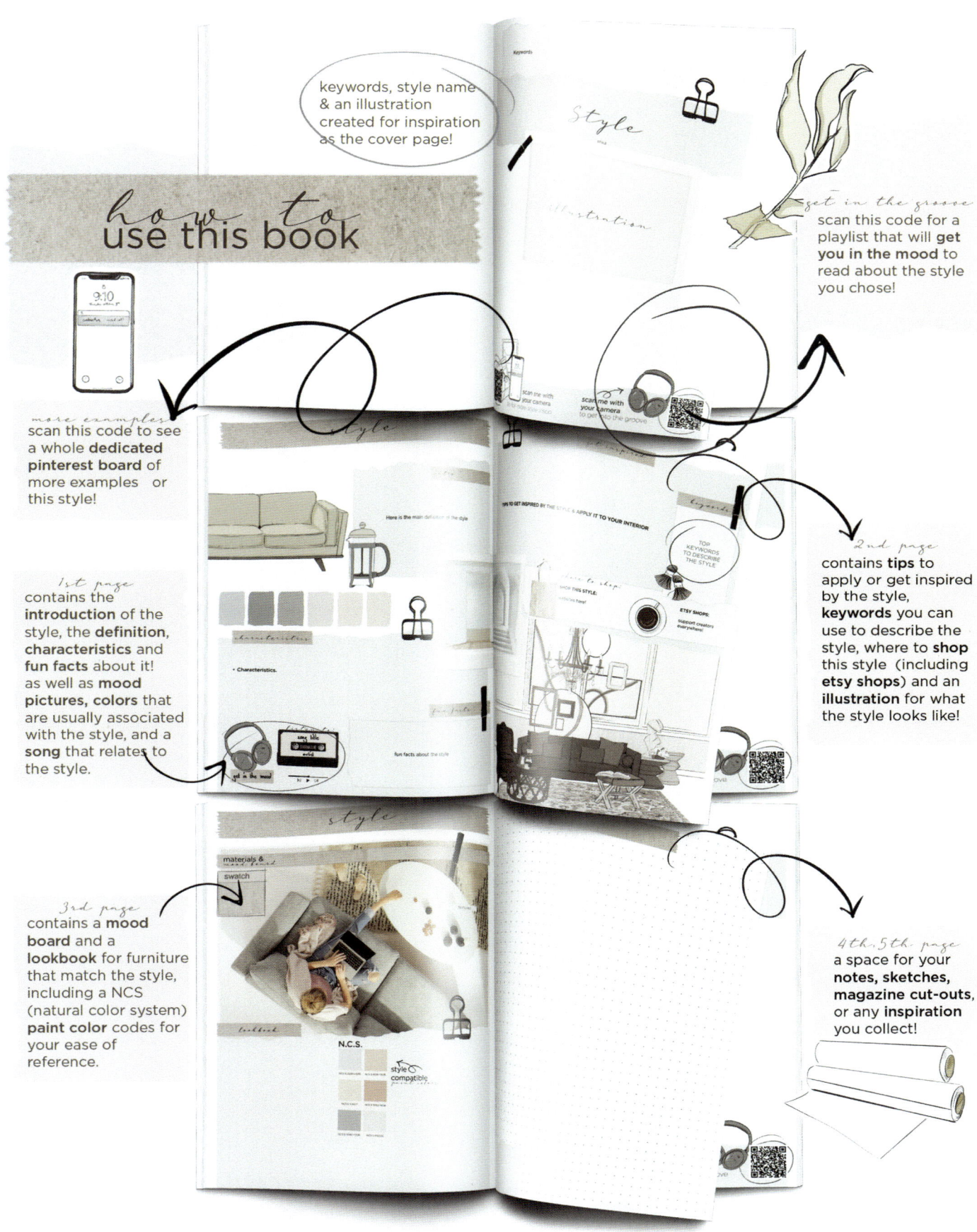

how to use this book

keywords, style name & an illustration created for inspiration as the cover page!

get in the groove
scan this code for a playlist that will **get you in the mood** to read about the style you chose!

more examples
scan this code to see a whole **dedicated pinterest board** of more examples or this style!

1st page
contains the **introduction** of the style, the **definition**, **characteristics** and **fun facts** about it! as well as **mood pictures, colors** that are usually associated with the style, and a **song** that relates to the style.

2nd page
contains **tips** to apply or get inspired by the style, **keywords** you can use to describe the style, where to **shop** this style (including **etsy shops**) and an **illustration** for what the style looks like!

3rd page
contains a **mood board** and a **lookbook** for furniture that match the style, including a NCS (natural color system) **paint color** codes for your ease of reference.

4th, 5th page
a space for your **notes, sketches, magazine cut-outs**, or any **inspiration** you collect!

Lush
Symmetrical
Grand
Decorated
Layered
Inviting

Arabian

ARABIAN

scan me with
your camera
to for more style inspo

9

scan me with
your camera
to get into the groove

arabian

The Arabian design is highly affected by the history of the architecture of the **Islamic world**. From rich decorative elements such as a variety of arches to the famous **geometric patterns** that are infused as an art form. Those patterns are applied generously to the architectural context as decorative elements. Currently, we see the Arabian style complimenting other styles. We often see it paired with more contemporary furniture while maintaining the rich motifs.

characteristics

- Pointed Arches, Play of Domes, Horseshoe Arches and Muqarnas Vaults as architectural elements. [1]
- Geometric patterns as an art form (Islamic architecture inspired) to conceal any sort of structure.
- Arabic Calligraphy as a part of the style.
- Foliation in forms like the classical vine and scroll motif.
- Rich Decorations, overall symmetry, and depth in Interiors created by a variety of scales.
- Play of lights through screens or windows.
- Similar space functions are gathered.
- Privacy is a big part of the style.
- Water features as a part of the design.

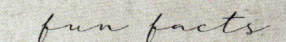

fun facts

- The Arabian Style is heavily defined by the Islamic architectural style, which is known for its geometrical shapes, structured layouts and grand proportions.
- The Interior of Burj Al Arab - Dubai follows the Arabian style. However, it is applied exaggeratedly and extravagantly to portray status and luxury.

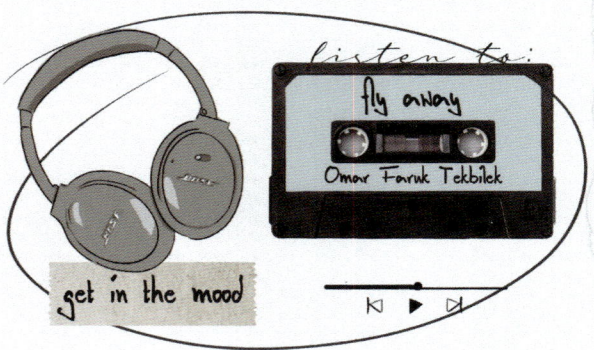

listen to:

fly away

Omar Faruk Tekbilek

get in the mood

If you want to pull off the Arabian style in your design (or simply infuse some Arabic touches in your space), here are some of the tips you can use:
- Utilize arches in their different forms in the space you are designing.
- Create a more symmetrical layout. Symmetry is a key to the style.
- Keep private areas concealed. Consider privacy in your design.
- Use geometry in flooring, in walls and decorative elements to your advantage.
- Keep the structural elements concealed to have a polished interior.
- Keep the light play interesting in the space through screens or windows.
- Use a variety of sizes with your pieces to induce more depth and luxury.

Lush
Symmetrical
Grand
Decorated
Layered
Inviting

where to shop:
pieces inspired by Arabic style:
https://theancienthome.com/
https://www.1stdibs.com/
http://www.ambiancefurnitures.com/
https://www.kashidadesign.com/

Etsy shops:
ArabianHomeDeco
HomeDecorbyJAD
ArabianHomeDeco

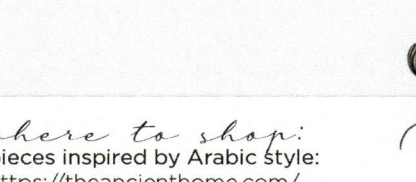

pointed arches

grandly scaled pieces

geometrical influences

materials &
mood board

mother of pearls

swatch

velvet

silver

ceramic tiles

look book

N.C.S.

style
compatible
paint colors

NCS S 0300-N   NCS S 3020-B40G

NCS S 3010-B90G   NCS S 7020-R80B

NCS S 5020-R80B   NCS S 3010-R80B

CUSHION:
Yellow Pillow Cover with
Islamic Geometrical
Pattern by: Vliving
on Etsy.com

STOOL:
Pair of Moorish/Islamic Open
Work Footstools with Mother
of Pearl Detail
1stdibs.com

DISPLAY CABINET:
Islamic Style Silvered Metal
and Glass Illuminated
Display Cabinet with
Shelves
1stdibs.com

SIDEBOARD:
Arabesque
Sideboard
kashidadesign.com

LIGHTING:
Oriental Lantern in
Copper and White
and Orange Glass,
circa 1970
1stdibs.com

CHAIR:
Aamaq
Long Chair
kashidadesign.com

SPACE FOR creativity

Geometric
Symmetrical
Sleek, Curvy
Contrasted
Sophisticated
Rich & Glamorous

Art Deco

ART DECO

scan me with
your camera
to for more style inspo

scan me with
your camera
to get into the groove

art deco

A very glamorous, elegant, functional and sophisticated style with **generous proportions,** expensive looking and rich in exotic materials[2]. The patterns and materials are exaggerated geometric, **lush** and abstracted. The style has been implemented also in a subdued fashion by maintaining the main characteristics of the style in an abstracted manner combined with simpler styles.

swatch

characteristics

• Lush, luxurious, theatrical and sophisticated by nature.
• Striking geometric boldness inspired by "trapezoidal, zigzagged, triangular shapes, chevron patterns, stepped forms, sweeping curves, and sunburst motifs - all of which can be found in every form of Art Deco, from furniture, buildings, jewelry, and fine art" [3]. Those are the most defining characteristics of the art deco era.
• Spaces are designed symmetrically.
• Sleek lines and simplistic forms that add high-impact visuals.
• Wooden furniture paired with metallic accents like chrome and brass hardware.
• Glass tops and reflective surfaces.
• Acute angles paired with curvier pieces.
• Metallic, high-gloss finishes

fun facts

• Art Deco was originally exhibited in 1925 during the "Exposition Internationale des Arts Decoratifs Industriels Modernes" in Paris, France.
• "Art Décoratif "is where the name Art Deco came from, which is a French phrase that means, you guessed it, Decorative Art.
• The set of the movie The Great Gatsby adapted the style beautifully to exhibit the style as a reference for its embodiment of luxury, status, and popularity.

listen to:
art deco
lanna del rey

get in the mood

If you want to pull off Art Deco style in your design (or simply infuse some glam in your space), here are some of the tips you can use:
• Don't be afraid of using geometric shapes on the walls, and the floor tiles.
• Infuse luxury into space by upholstering or covering your walls with lush textiles like velvet.
• Use curvy furniture pieces on a grand scale.
• Enrich the furniture pieces with vertical channel tufting as it is very common in the art-deco inspired furniture pieces
• Create a symmetrical layout to achieve a classical look.
• Glam is channeled in accessories and brass metals.
• Keep your lighting as a focal point that fits the profile of the style. A delicious level of drama can be maintained by adding crystal chandeliers and wall sconces that are inspired by the geometrical approach.
• Look for pieces that have saboted legs with metallic finishes.
• Utilize expensive and exotic materials, veneers, lacquers, and textiles.

keywords

Geometric
Symmetrical
Sleek, Curvy
Contrasted
Sophisticated
Rich & Glamorous

Wesley Tingey
@wesleyphotography

where to shop:
Vintage & modernized pieces inspired by art deco:
https://artdecocollection.com/
https://www.muranti.com/
https://www.cb2.com/
https://www.kare-design.com/
https://www.westelm.com/

Etsy shops:
CristherArt
GlossaryDepotVintage
Coloritto
Spoonflower
TimelessDecorations

geometric shapes
brass finishes

lush velvet vertical
channel tufted

curvilinear sofa

art deco

materials & mood board

swatch — shark skin

swatch — velvet

mahogany

jade

silver

ivory

mirrors

look book

CUSHION
Marble Art Deco
Tiles in Soft Pastels
by Spoonflower

CHAIR
Roar & Rabbit™
Pleated Swivel
Chair
westelm.com

N.C.S.

style compatible paint colors

NCS S 0300-N

NCS S 2005-Y70R

NCS S 6005-B80G

NCS S 4550-Y90R

NCS S 5040-R

NCS S 4010-B90G

LIGHTING:
West Elm
westelm.com

MIRROR:
H&M Home

SIDE TABLE:
Curve Gold Side
Table - CB2
Exclusive

SOFA:
ART DECO SOFA Ruby by: Muranti

18

Creativity

Exaggerated
Asymmetrical
Organic Lines
Heavily Ornamented
Artistic

Art Nouveau

ART NOUVEAU

scan me with
your camera
to for more style inspo

scan me with
your camera
to get into the groove

art nouveau

swatch

Art Nouveau is inspiring to many designers currently because of it's courageous, daring, and exuberant presence. While it's rare right now for an interior space to be designed with art nouveau as the main style, it remains an inspiration to artists and designers. This inspiration is usually borrowed from the confident lines, naturalistic ornaments, fabrics, and colors which are used as accents in more "eclectic" spaces. Moreover, the style can be mixed with traditional or with contemporary elements.

Lāsma Artmane
Clarsmann

characteristics

- Rich in patterns. Naturalistic by default.
- Exaggeration in form with fantasy-like [4] spaces that are filled with energy.
- Resolutely asymmetrical in every shape and form.
- Organic shapes that are curvilinear inspired by botanical designs which are not only present in the furniture and accessories, but also ingrained in the architectural context. Making the room feel less generic and more like a sculptural masterpiece.
- Beautifying all objects with ornaments and decorations.
- Merging between art, architecture, and interior design.
- Jewel-tones as a color palette
- "Whiplash" curves. [5]

fun facts

listen to:

solace

scott joplin, martin sowler

get in the mood

- Art Nouveau is considered to be the first "modern" style between about 1890 and 1910
- "Art Nouveau translates into "New Art" in French
- The set of the movie "Chéri" adapted the style to convey a romantic undertone.

22

To get inspired by Art Nouveau style:
• Add a few organic curvy architectural elements subtly. The style is super bold and going overboard with it is easy to do.
• Maintain an asymmetrical layout. Asymmetry is the heart of Art Nouveau.
• Indulge in the jewel-tone color palette.
• Keep the pieces you use in the design daring and unique.
• Treat your space as a sculptural masterpiece and infuse it with curvilinear asymmetrical patterns that are inspired by natural motifs like nymphs, peacocks, dragonflies, irises, waves, and other botanical forms.
• Utilize wooden vintage pieces of furniture as carved wooden furniture is heavily used in the style.

exaggerated asymmetrical organic lines heavily ornamented **artistic.**

where to shop:
Vintage & modernized pieces inspired by art nouveau:
https://www.1stdibs.com/furniture/style/art-nouveau/
https://www.macklowegallery.com/
https://www.chairish.com/style/art-nouveau
https://www.dorisleslieblau.com/

Etsy shops:
BeyondtheBeatenPath
Artgaze
ArtNationByJames
Imagesdesign
Cute Miniatures:
ArjenSpinhovenMiniat

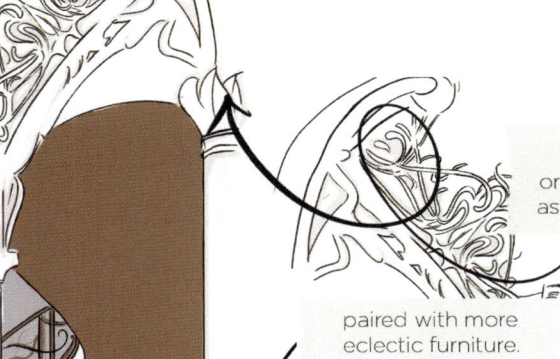

the iconic "whiplash" ornaments can be used as an accent in the style

paired with more eclectic furniture.

carved-wooden elements

art nouveau

materials & mood board

swatch

Wildwood Flower - Lt Olive,
Morris & Company

ceramics

carved wood

cast iron

William Morris   William Morris

"Humbert & Poyet" image by Francis Amiand.

stained glass

teak

walnut

oak

look book

N.C.S.

NCS S 4030-Y50R	NCS S 4010-G10Y
NCS S 1010-Y70R	NCS S 4050-Y70R
NCS S 6010-G10Y	NCS S 1005-G40Y

style compatible *paint colors*

CUSHION
Old Art Reborn for
Zazzle.com

LIGHTING
Sullivan Colourful
Tiffany Art Noveau
Ceiling Pendant
bespokelights.co.uk

TILE:
William De Morgan
Reproduction Decorative
Ceramic Wall Tile
By: Imagesdesign
on Etsy.Com

TABLE:
French Art Nouveau
Table by
Edouard Colonna

BENCH:
Antoni Gaudi Casa Batlló
Bench Manufactured by BD in
Solid Varnished Oak

RUG:
Vintage Viennese Art
Nouveau Carpet
dorisleslieblau.com

Creativity

Dynamic
Artistic
Home-Made
Layered
Free-Spirited

Bohemian

BOHEMIAN

scan me with
your camera
to for more style inspo

scan me with
your camera
to get into the groove

bohemian

The bohemian style is a tribute to creative and **free-spirited** souls. It's a global style where the room is filled with souvenirs from **travels** and heirlooms. There are absolutely no rules in the style. While you can go with a wild and bold color palette, you can also go with a super neutral palette where the wild side lays in textures and thrift-store furniture pieces. You often contrast the hand-made materials (like burlap, sisal, and crocheted items) with higher-end silks, cotton, and chenille. Both hanging plants and floor plants play an important role as plants are an essential part of the style. Furniture pieces are usually one of a kind.

characteristics

- Normally paints a picture of travelers, hippies, artists, and "free spirits." [6]
- A dynamic style that is filled with life.
- Layered patterns, textures, and prints. A "More is more" approach.
- A simpler foundation where the character is infused in the furniture and accessories.
- Bold colors (not exclusively) and pattern dominated furnishings. [7]
- Void of structure or rules, often chaotic and artistic.
- Furniture is unique, vintage, and obtained from thrifting. Fabrics are slightly worn.
- Fringe, crochet, macramé, and burlap are contrasted against more luxurious fabrics like higher-end silk and chenille. [8]
- Plenty of plants, life thrives in this style.
- Home-made feel and natural textures fill the space.

fun facts

- The essence of "boho" culture is to live carefree, and look the opposite of precise or clean, which means having no rules.
- The Bohemian Style is one of the most searched Interior Design styles on Google!

listen to:

bohemian rhapsody

Queen

get in the mood

Tips to get inspired by the Bohemian style:
• You can go with a couple of different approaches with the Boho style because there are no particular rules. As an example, you can keep a simple base making it look less cluttered, or you can go on to a more colorful approach if that's your style.
• Thrift the pieces of furniture from vintage stores or your travels if you are a frequent traveler.
• Use macramé and fringe in your space, it indicates that you have the bohemian style in mind as it became a signature move in boho spaces.
• Do not be afraid of layering patterns and using colorful prints and attachments. Tassels and fringes are usually used in bohemian accessories.
• Use natural materials like sisal and burlap against more luxurious materials, a contrast in texture is very common.
• Fill the space with plants in different positions.

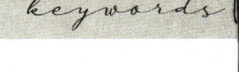

keywords

Dynamic
Artistic
Home-Made
Layered
Free-Spirited

where to shop:

To find some Bohemian style pieces, visit:
https://www.anthropologie.com/
https://www.urbanoutfitters.com/
https://froy.com/
https://www.kathykuohome.com/
https://www.maisonsdumonde.com/

Etsy Shops:
paisleyandpolkaspots
KamalnathHandicraft
HandmadeLoveCrafts
MadeByMegMacrame
CoastalBohoStudio

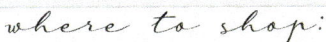

macramé mixed with thriving plant life

pop of color mixed in with neutrals

layered rugs and patterns

bohemian

materials & *mood board*

swatch

linen

natural fibers

light wood

textures

lookbook

N.C.S.

NCS S 2030-Y50R	NCS S 1505-Y60R
NCS S 1002-Y	NCS S 2010-Y60R
NCS S 5040-Y70R	NCS S 1000-N

style **compatible** *paint colors*

RUG
Red Bohemian
Area Rug Carpet
by Persian Area Rugs
on Amazon.com

LIGHTING
Safavieh Lighting
Whitley
overstock.com

CHAIR
Peacock Chair in Rattan
by Kouboo
on amazon.com

BAR STOOL
Randall Wicker
Bar Stool
froy.com

MACRAME
Wall Hanging Shelf Cotton
Rope Wood Hanger Tapestry
BLUETTEK on amazon.com

SOFA
BOLCHOÏ
2/3-Seater Multicolor
Cotton Sofa
maisonsdumonde.com

SPACE FOR creativity

Relaxed
Natural Elements
Beach Inspired
Light
Breezy
Casual
Clutter-Free

Coastal

COASTAL

scan me with
your camera
to for more style inspo

scan me with
your camera
to get into the groove

swatch

swatch

The Coastal Style is a derivative of the nautical style [9] but in a subtler and more minimalistic way. If you like fresh-looking, beachy, casual and light-hearted spaces, then this style is for you. Spaces are filled with light and often bring the outside environment in. This style is especially applied in beach houses. Materials are relaxed like loose linens and are natural like jute, seagrass, and straw. Accessories have a sea-side soul to them and are used to hint at the style rather than clutter the space with it.

characteristics

- Natural, light, breezy, and open spaces with clean aesthetics.
- Linens and light airy fabrics.
- Light wooden tones, mainly white-washed wood.
- Seagrass and natural materials are used.
- Less is more, especially with colors. Light neutral palette with accents of ocean-inspired colors.
- Casual and comfortable furniture pieces, mainly slip-covered sofas.
- Sea-side accessories are used in moderation.
- Clutter-free with a simple base.

fun facts

- The coastal style takes a hint from the natural elements of a beachy scenery, the balance, breeziness, and subtlety of it all.
- Architectural Digest took us on a tour in Actress Margot Robbie production company LuckyChap's in Los Angeles which was designed in a coastal-chic style, to see the tour, scan this code right here

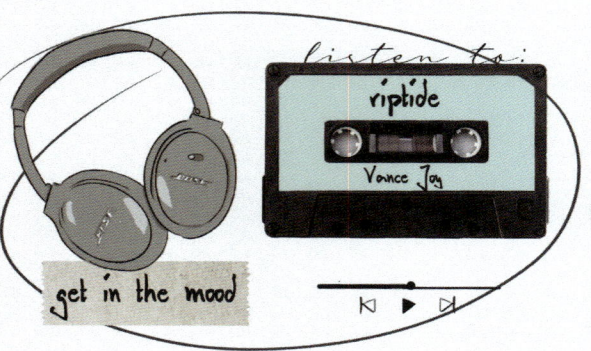

listen to:

riptide

Vance Joy

get in the mood

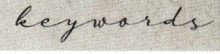

To get inspired by the Coastal style, use the following tips:
• Plan an open space, it's all about the flow and breeziness in the room.
• Apply a light neutral color scheme with hints of ocean-inspired accents.
• Bring the outside in and take hints from the seaside, but do not go overboard with it, remember that less is more in coastal style.
• Do not be afraid to use bigger scale furniture pieces. Causal and comfortable pieces are the core of a coastal-inspired interior.
• Bring in slip-covered furniture alongside with rattan, sisal, light-washed woods, and glass to complete the look.
• Linens and breezy fabrics are the go-to in Coastal style interiors.
•Add Tropical plants to bring life to the room.

Relaxed
Natural Elements
Beach Inspired
Light
Breezy
Casual
Clutter-Free

where to shop:

To find some coastal-inspired pieces, visit:
https://www.potterybarn.com/
https://www.overstock.com/
https://www.cottageandbungalow.com/
https://thebeachfurniture.com.au/

Etsy shops:
TheSailorAndMermaid
DriftwoodAndPebbles
MyBeachsideStyle

sea-side inspired
accessories

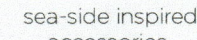

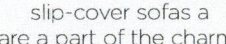

light, breezy and simple

slip-cover sofas a
are a part of the charm

coastal

materials & mood board

white wash

ash wood

rope

glass

lookbook

swatch — linen

swatch — rattan

N.C.S.

NCS S 510-B10G	NCS S 0300-N
NCS S 1005-Y60R	NCS S 0510-B70G
NCS S 020-B10G	NCS S 1000-N

style compatible *paint colors*

WALLPAPER:
Elizabeth Robinson
wallsneedlove.com

COFFEE TABLE:
Enfield Coffee Table
Beachcrest Home on
Wayfair

LIGHTING:
HENDAYE
maisonsdumonde.com

ROOM DIVIDER:
Walton 4 Panel
Room Divider
wayfair.co.uk

POUF
Braided Jute
CB2.com

DECORATIVE OBJECTS :
Faux White Coral
Double Loop Knot
CB2.com

SOFA:
FÄRLÖV 3-Seater Slip-Cover
Sofa - IKEA.com

creativity

Simple & Basic
Open Plans
Modular
Solid
Subtle Sophistication
Sleek & Fresh

Contemporary

CONTEMPORARY

scan me with
your camera
to for more style inspo

scan me with
your camera
to get into the groove

contemporary

The contemporary style is the "**current** style" in today's interior design world. It is defined by simplicity, **subtle sophistication**, intentional use of texture, and **clean lines** [10]. If you find yourself admiring the modern style, but also like to keep up with trends [10], then contemporary is your go-to style. This is because it embraces the neutral color palettes and simplistic forms with layouts that are built around open plans, bigger windows, and sleek lines, without neglecting touches of nature. What makes the contemporary style special is the fact that it is comfortable and welcoming without being cluttered and dark.[10]

swatch

characteristic

• Strong visible lines for furniture and accessories.
• Features of recessed lighting.
• Metals, stones, and opaque or clear glass accent.
• Bold statement pieces paired with simple and uncluttered space.
• Natural fibers, wools, cotton, linens, silks, and jute.
• Basic, bare, bold and structured.
• Has elements of modernism, postmodernism, de-constructivism, art deco, futurism, etc, with a "less is more" approach
• White, cream, beige, brown or gray. The accent can be put also on bold color schemes as long as they comply with the already established balance.
• Softer than completely Modern design.
• Larger windows and open plans.

listen to:
everything i wanted
Billie Eilish

get in the mood

fun facts

• The Contemporary style is a current style, which means it's constantly changing.
• Harvey Specter's office in the T.V. show: Suits, follows the contemporary style.
• Ashley Tracey and Laura McLellan renovated a traditional interior into a contemporary one with touches of traditional, watch them talk about the details by scanning this code:

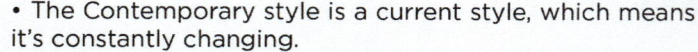

Tips to get inspired by the Contemporary Style:
• Maintain strong lines throughout the design, in architectural elements, window frames, furniture, wall art, and sculpture. [10]
• Keep a neutral color scheme, and opt for an accent color if you want to mix it up.
• Borrow elements that are trendy from different styles, as this style is ever-changing. Keeping up with trends is important.
• Design with an open-space intent, blurring the division between spaces, open spaces are the core of a contemporary home.
• Opt for furniture pieces with clean lines, without adornment or carvings. But rather simple lines. [11]
• Look for texture instead of pattern, enhance the space with pieces that have a natural texture visible.
• Less is more, add hidden storage to the spaces, detain the space of the clutter.
• Focus on key accent accessories instead of knick-knacks everywhere.

keywords

Simple & Basic
Open Plans
Neutral
Modular
Solid
Subtle Sophistication
Sleek & Fresh

where to shop:
To find some contemporary pieces, visit:
https://designitch.com/
https://www.allmodern.com/
https://www.indigo-living.com/
https://www.cb2.com/
https://www.westelm.com/
https://www.boconcept.com/

Etsy Shops:
canvasbrushesknives
MarolizanaPillows
SnoogsAndWilde
ReupholsteredStudio

interesting accent pieces

clean line for furniture

textured and solid textiles

41

swatch

suede

swatch

leather

steel

materials &
mood board

metals

glass

N.C.S.

lookbook

COFFEE TABLE
Drum Storage
Coffee Table
West Elm

NCS S 0300-N   NCS S 0500-N

NCS S 9000-N   NCS S 4000-N

NCS S 8500-N   NCS S 1000-N

style
compatible
paint colors

LIGHTING
Champignon
6-Light Chandelier
West Elm

CONSOLE
Pinehurst Console
Table
AllModern

ACCENT CHAIR
FLO armchair
brown
The One

SOFA
Essentiel Sofa
by SABA ITALIA for
Designitch

Creativity

Contrasted
Coherent
Bold
Mixed Styles
Quirky
Risky

Eclectic

ECLECTIC

scan me with
your camera
to for more style inspo

scan me with
your camera
to get into the groove

eclectic

swatch

The Eclectic style is very true to its name. It's a **cohesive mix** between architectural elements that varies from extremely contemporary to extremely traditional designed with elements from different periods and styles. Usually, there is one dominant style that creates a more **pulled-together** look. It's not an easy style to pull off, but it is also, a style that is infused with personality, rooms that are created with the eclectic style in mind are always one-of-a-kind.

Allie Smith
@alliecoffeeandpassport

characteristics

- Purposeful and functional, doesn't adhere to one style.
- Harmonious in mixing between different interior design periods and styles.
- Unforeseen combinations of architectural features, furniture, and accessories.
- Rich in both rough and smooth textures, alongside patterns.
- Asymmetrical and daring layouts.
- Bold, playful & quirky.
- High in contrast.
- Unique items with sentimental value.

fun facts

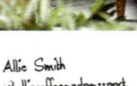

listen to:
eclectic prawn
dumbo gets mad

get in the mood

• In the award-winning movie, La La Land, we can see the Eclectic style in the house where Mia (Emma Stone) lives with her friends, mixing styles like Retro, Mid-Century Modern and Contemporary together.

•Tour An Eclectic SoHo Loft by Michele Varian covered by House&Home

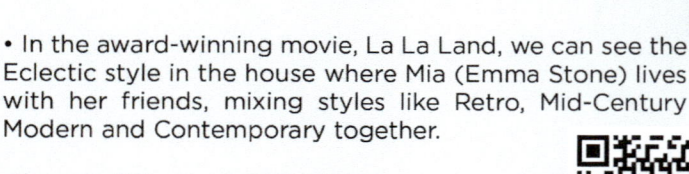

Tips to get inspired by the eclectic style:
• Be bold in your choices, but look for items that have something in common like textures, patterns, materials, or colors.
• Experiment with different patterns, textures, and accessories. To make the room look more cohesive, repeat the same texture or pattern in multiple locations throughout the space.
• Take risks with colors, but keep some void for the eye to rest. Balance is key.
• With that being said, pick a color scheme at the beginning of the project with a dominant color in mind to avoid a cluttered look.
• Utilize the contrast of elements.
• Maintain one dominant style to keep a pleasing aesthetic.
• Add artworks that contain the color palette of the room to tie everything up.

keywords

Contrasted
Coherent
Bold
Mixed Styles
Quirky
Risky

Allie Smith
@alliecoffeeandpassport

where to shop:
To find some eclectic style pieces, visit:
https://www.gilt.com/
https://www.roseandgrey.co.uk/
https://www.made.com/
https://www.kartell.com/
https://www.spoonflower.com/

Etsy shops:
ThriftysRetro
JunkYardMutz
ChaosandWonderDesign
ModernHomeEclectic
TreasureOfHandicraft

contrast between contemporary and traditional

some neutral colors to ease the style up

quirky, bold colors on classical silhouette

eclectic

materials & *mood board*

swatch — *velvet*

swatch — nylon

carrara marble

look book

acrylic

metals

mixed metals

N.C.S.

NCS S 0300-N	NCS S 1015-R10B
NCS S 3020-B70G	NCS S 2050-Y80R
NCS S 2050-R10B	NCS S 5540-R70B

style compatible *paint colors*

CHEST OF DRAWER
Mid-Century Geometric Hand
Painted Chest Of Drawers
by ALPHA FLEUR
www.notonthehighstreet.com

COFFEE TABLE
Ashiko coffee table silver
www.moeshomecollection.com

DINING CHAIR
Lennox dining
chair green-m2
www.moeshome
collection.com/

LIGHTING
TIMOTHEE
Maisons Du Monde

SOFA
Kooper 2 Seater
Sofa
Made.com

48

SPACE FOR creativity

Cozy & Rustic
Relaxed
Light
Neutral
Lived-In
Personal
Handmade

Farmhouse

FARMHOUSE

**scan me with
your camera**
to for more style inspo

**scan me with
your camera**
to get into the groove

farmhouse

swatch

The Farmhouse style fixates on **natural elements** that are cozy, full of life, and warm. Celebrating accessories and **heirlooms** in every corner, with furniture pieces that are of considerable size, decorated with different patterns that feel inviting to utilize. At present, it is being paired with the modern style taking on a neutral color palette to keep the style from looking dated.

characteristics

- Cozy, rustic and full of character.
- Hand-made feel, crafted pieces.
- Wrapped in wood and wooden panelings.
- Traditional French doors and windows.
- Light and relaxed.
- Bigger furniture pieces.
- Inviting space, lots of accessories, heirlooms, and personal items.
- Open shelving and display cabinets.
- Linens and natural blends for fabrics.
- A neutral, light color palette, with warmer natural accents.
- Elements that you find in a cottage used as accessories.

fun facts

listen to:

meant to be

Bebe Rexha feat. F.G.L.

get in the mood

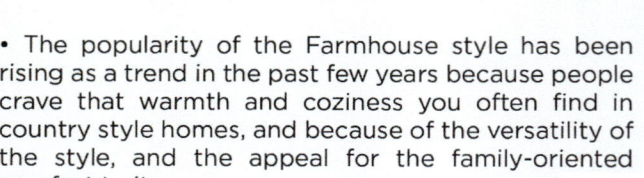

- The popularity of the Farmhouse style has been rising as a trend in the past few years because people crave that warmth and coziness you often find in country style homes, and because of the versatility of the style, and the appeal for the family-oriented comfort to it.
- Watch Sharrah from The Kinwoven Home channel shopping for Farmhouse style!

52

Tips to get inspired by the farmhouse style:

• Consider using shiplap as your wall treatment. Usually, white-wash wood paneling is ideal.

• Do not shy away from using larger pieces of furniture.

• Show personality through accessories that are inspired by a farmhouse, rustic elements that complete the look.

• Use linens and cotton, even jute to bring the outside in, natural elements that you find in a farm, or that are inspired by the color, texture or pattern.

• Use black metal instead of gold and silver.

• Wooden accents everywhere to enhance the farmhouse feel

• Add botanicals (faux or real) like ficus, olive tree, boxwood wreath and sage plant to add life to the room.

keywords

Cozy & Rustic
Relaxed
Light
Neutral
Lived-In
Personal
Handmade

where to shop:
To find some farmhouse style pieces, visit:
https://www.potterybarn.com/
https://www.hayneedle.com/
https://www.ashleyfurniture.com/
https://www.worldmarket.com/
https://www.restorationhardware.com/

Etsy Shops:
ATZHomeDesign
higginshomedecor
TwistedBobbinDesigns
designstylebymarci
SimplyRusticbyJanet

shiplap as a wall treatment

family

white-wash distressed wood

178

untreated wooden accents

farmhouse

swatch
linens

swatch
burlap

reclaimed wood

distressed wood

materials &
mood board

metals

rattan

N.C.S.

NCS S 0300-N	NCS S 2005-B80G
NCS S 2005-G50Y	NCS S 1505-Y20R
NCS S 1000-N	NCS S 8500-N

style
compatible
paint colors

lookbook

COFFEE TABLE
Parquet Reclaimed
Wood Round
Coffee Table
Pottery Barn

LIGHTING
Champignon Suri
Chandelier
Pottery Barn

DINING CHAIR
Natural Linen Paige
Round Back Dining
Chairs
World Market

ROCKING CHAIR
Ivory Joanna
Rocking Chair
World Market

SOFA
Carlisle Upholstered
Sofa
Pottery Barn

54

SPACE FOR Creativity

Elegant
Dramatic
Luxurious
Glamorous
Classic

Hollywood Regency

HOLLYWOOD REGENCY

scan me with
your camera
to for more style inspo

scan me with
your camera
to get into the groove

The most **sophisticated** and **dramatic** style. Hollywood Regency is a glamourous, shiny and luxurious style. From dramatic accent walls to velvety-tufted sofas, it's undeniably **extravagant**. It borrows the main lines from other styles like Art Deco and Mid-Century Modern while adding an expensive flair to them. You will often find shiny materials and surfaces glittering in the Hollywood Regency style interior.

characteristics

- An extremely extravagant, dramatic, moody, sophisticated, and luxurious style.
- Shiny surfaces, mirrors, and metals play a major role, high gloss materials such as natural marbles are used heavily.
- Furniture pieces that borrow the aesthetics of Art Deco & Mid-Century Modern are utilized.
- Bold color-blocking contrasts that often involve black and white patterns, inspired by the baroque style.
- Classical furniture silhouettes that are made in more contemporary materials.
- Tufted furniture pieces are also a key to the style especially with velvet in a myriad of hues from, subtle to strong. [12]
- Crystal, marble, stone, and high-shine décor pieces and accessories.
- Touchable glamour, textiles are plush like satin, silk, fur, leather, and of course
- Emphasis on the details such as nailhead trims and edge trims on furniture.

listen to:
hollywood forever
FINNEAS

get in the mood

- One of the biggest names who currently dominated the Hollywood Regency style is the American designer: Kelly Wearstler.
- Watch more about the Hollywood Regency style by Erikka Dawn Interiors on YouTube here:

Elegant
Dramatic
Luxurious
Glamorous
Classic

Tips to get inspired by the Hollywood Regency style:
• Keep wall treatments luxurious, wall trims and moldings visible, as well as using patterned wallpaper on accent walls.
• Look for high-quality full of details pieces of furniture in luxurious finishes.
• Do not be afraid to use shiny metals and surfaces, opt for touchable glamour such as plush textiles and high-end materials.
• Maintain a bold color palette, but keep your palette small and cohesive, while you need to inject color and have high contrast in the space, it's better to keep your color palette limited to 4 colors max.
• Mix classic patterns and solid colors.

where to shop:

To find some Hollywood Regency style pieces, visit:
https://www.chairish.com/
https://www.1stdibs.com/
https://www.kathykuohome.com/
https://www.restorationhardware.com/
https://www.pier1.com/

Etsy Shops:
OKERvintage
AylasFineGoods
JulieSimpleRedesign
IAMMVV

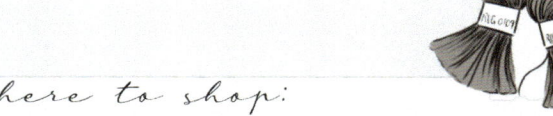

high-contrast

luxurios and dramatic furnishings

geometric luxurious tiles

hollywood regency

swatch

velvet

golden accents

lookbook

MIRROR
Eichholtz Mulini
Hollywood Regency
Amber
kathykuohome.com

STOOL
Lorna Regency
White Faux Fur
Antique Gold Stool
kathykuohome.com

N.C.S.

NCS S 4010-Y10R   NCS S 9000-N

NCS S 8010-B90G   NCS S 8500-N

NCS S 7020-R30B   NCS S 1000-N

style
compatible
paint colors

LIGHTING
Amelie Crystal
Chandelier
zinhome.com

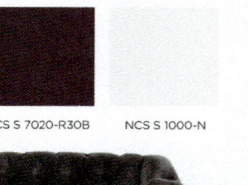

SIDE TABLE
Tiff Hollywood
Regency End Table
kathykuohome.com

SOFA
Damon Grey Velvet
Rolled Arm Tufted Sofa
zinhome.com

BOOKCASE
Helena Staggered Antique
Brass + Glass Shelf
Bookcase
zinhome.com

SIDEBOARD
Theodore Alexander
Sideboard
kathykuohome.com

Creativity

Unfinished
Raw
Lofty
Uncluttered
Open

Industrial

scan me with
your camera
to for more style inspo

scan me with
your camera
to get into the groove

industrial

intro

The Industrial style is defined by the **finished-unfinished** lofty-warehouses type of look. The **juxtaposition** of sleek modern pieces versus exposed architectural structures, **reclaimed** materials, and leathers make for a deep, layered and weirdly cohesive look, resulting in a space that is full of character.

The architectural structure of the typical industrial-style space is exposed and even highlighted. Beams, ducts, and pipes are visible, treatments like bare bricks and concrete flooring are heavily used. Paired with minimal use of accessories.

characteristics

- Open plans and layouts. Lofty-look of warehouses and factories. [13]
- Exposed beam, pipes, and ducts.
- Raw materials such as concrete flooring and bare brick walls.
- Unfinished looking interior-architecture paired with sleek, modern furniture pieces.
- Minimal approach with accessories in the space that are interesting conversation-starter pieces.
- Raw materials such as galvanized metal, glass, leathers, and reclaimed woods.
- Highlight pipe-structured furniture pieces paired with reclaimed woods. [14]
- Neutral colors such as blacks, greys, and browns.

fun facts

- The Humphrey residence in the show Gossip Girl has a strong industrial style influence.

To learn more about Industrial Interior Design in 2020, watch Ula Burgiel on YouTube:

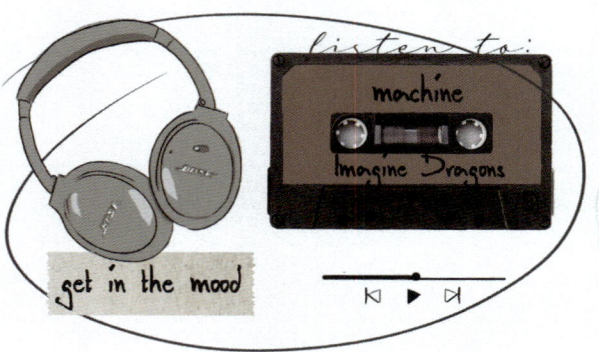

listen to:

machine
Imagine Dragons

get in the mood

Tips to apply the industrial style:
• Keep an open floor plan. Get inspired by warehouses and factories when creating the layout.
• Leave the structural elements in the space exposed, bricks, beams, ducts, and pipes are all a part of the charm of the style.
• Opt for concrete, cement, or a reclaimed wooden planks flooring finish.
• Look for furniture that has galvanized metals mixed with reclaimed wood furniture pieces with pipe-structure.
• Modern and Mid-Century Modern style furniture pieces are also a part of the style.
• Do not clutter the space with accessories, add only functional accessories or conversation-starters.
• If you have the height for it, opt for a mezzanine to create a lofty look.

keywords

Unfinished
Raw
Lofty
Uncluttered
Open

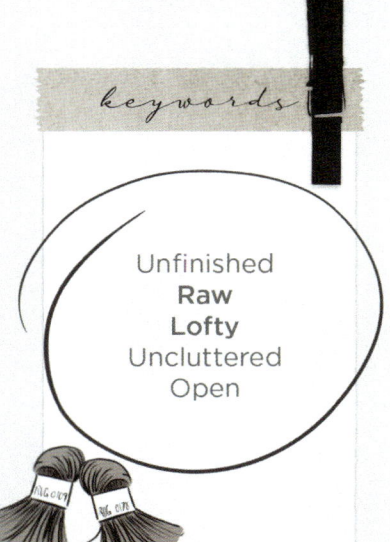

where to shop:

To find some industrial style pieces, visit:
https://www.bellacor.com/
https://froy.com/
https://www.maisonsdumonde.com/
https://ikea.com/
https://www.overstock.com/

Etsy Shops:
SilverBeardLampCo
IndustEvo
BearCreekproducts

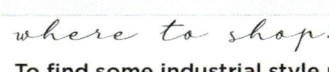

raw finishes
exposed structure

rustic feel to the pieces
lots of texture

concrete flooring

materials &
mood board

swatch

leather

metal

lookbook

N.C.S.

NCS S 6005-Y50R   NCS S 9000-N

NCS S 1002-Y   NCS S 8000-N

NCS S 6040-Y70R   NCS S 1000-N

style
compatible
paint colors

RUG
Red Bohemian
Area Rug Carpet
by Persian Area Rugs
on Amazon.com

BASKET
BORSTAD
IKEA.com

LIGHTING
Dazhuan Industrial Light
Fixture Ceiling Pendant
by Dazhuan
on Amazon.com

SHELF
JONAS - Industrial-Style Pine
and Aged-Effect Metal
Shelving Unit
maisonsdumonde.com

BAR STOOL
KULLABERG
Stool, pine,
black
IKEA.com

SOFA
Brown Antwerp Sofa
bellacor.com

STORAGE UNIT
ROOSEVELT
maisonsdumonde.com

creativity

Balanced
Asymmetrical
Natural
Structured
Minimalistic
Clean Lines
Negative Space

Japanese

JAPANESE

scan me with
your camera
to for more style inspo

scan me with
your camera
to get into the groove

japanese

swatch

intro

Japanese style is considered very specific to the culture of the Japanese people. However, a lot of designers get a lot of inspiration by how serene and beautiful the Japanese style is, so they mix it with more contemporary elements. Characterized by **lighter visual weight**, whether it comes to the colors or the way interiors are furnished. "Natural" is a very important keyword, as it draws its inspiration from the surrounding nature, it affects the interior where you find a lot of lighter woods mixed, usually muted colors, lighter fabrics, and grid-elements.

Reinaldo Kevin
@reinaldokevin

characteristics

- Serene, peaceful, and Zen.
- Minimalistic elements.
- Balanced asymmetry.
- Negative spaces with a void to relax the eyes.
- Clean looking architectural context.
- A mix of woods, sisal, and other natural materials.
- Floor seating, humble functionality.
- Natural materials like light stone, blond woods, pebbles, bamboo.
- Simplicity, clean lines, usually modular designs.
- Linens and light fabrics.
- Motifs that directly relate to the culture.

fun facts

• The "Shoji" is a translucent paper that is usually used in the interior and exterior doors in the Japanese houses instead of glass. It is what gives this unique blurred soft shadows to the Japanese interior because of how it lets the light in. 15
• The "Fusuma" is the Japanese term they call sliding panels that function as both doors and walls in the Japanese interior. Their main role is to create a flexible division within the room.

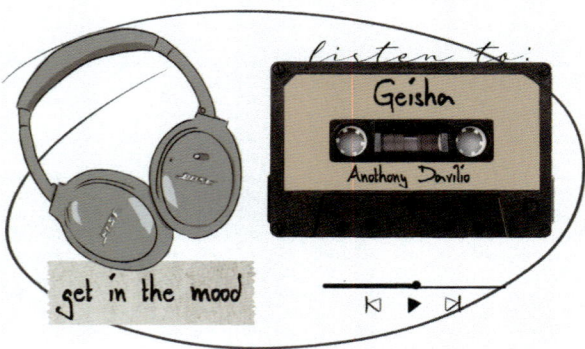

listen to:
Geisha
Anthony Davilio

get in the mood

70

A lot of people find inspiration from the simplicity of the Japanese style, the lightness of the visual weight, the natural materials, and the grid that is always associated with it, here is how you can get inspired by it too:

• Use louvers or partitions that align with the style of the Japanese door to divide your functional spaces. You can also utilize sliding panels as room dividers, or to create more flexibility in space.
• Mix light woods with other natural materials like bamboo and sisal.
• Prioritize natural lighting. An open space with soft shadows is a beautiful detail that works a mood booster, a great addition to the interior.
• Modular furniture is one of the stables in the style, because of the simplicity of those pieces.
• Do not be afraid of the negative space, the Japanese style is famous for voids that function as a relaxing break to the eye.

keywords

Balanced
Asymmetrical
Natural
Structured
Minimalistic
Clean Lines
Negative Space

where to shop:

Shops inspired by Japanese interiors:
https://www.muji.com/
https://www.haikudesigns.com/
https://muku-store.com/
https://ookkuu.com/

Etsy shops:
Bee9designshop
DeccoPrint
FutonTokoyo
Ruhodesign

Wesley Tingey
@wesleyphotography

paper panels for dividing spaces.

natural materials and simplicty of form

traditional floor seating

materials &
mood board

swatch

linen

beech wood

ash wood

N.C.S.

lookbook

COFFEE TABLE:
CAM coffee table
interiorsonline.com

FLOOR CUSHION
TEIXIDORS
Thor Ecological Merino
Wool Floor Cushion
selfridges.com

NCS 0300-N   NCS S2005-Y70R

NCS S 0502-Y50R   NCS S 3005-G80Y

NCS S 8000-N   NCS S 1505-Y10R

style
compatible
paint colors

PLATFORM BED:
Arata Japanese Platform Bed
haikudesigns.com

LIGHTING:
Lantern Pendant
finnishdesignshop.com

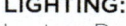

BONSAI:
@seasonsfloristry

ROOM DIVIDER:
Living Space
Bamboo Folding
Screen
ACE Hardware

Screativity

Comfortable
Luxurious but Raw
Spontaneous
Nature-Inspired
Artsy

Mediterranean

MEDITERRANEAN

scan me with
your camera
to for more style inspo

75

scan me with
your camera
to get into the groove

mediterranean

swatch

intro

The Mediterranean style is all about evoking the coastal feel of the European countries, terra cotta, stone and geometric Lisbon **patterned tiles** that are tied together with wrought iron, and muted shades of colors that complement the rough elements of stucco walls paired with translucent fabrics are why this style has a soft, romantic quality to it.

characteristics

• Luxurious and comfortable.
• Influenced by the European eloquence rustic décor paired with aqua blue and earthy tones combined with modern, traditional, and contemporary elements. [16]
• Bold patterns with simple lines that repeat throughout space.
• Smoothly warm color palette juxtaposed with ocean-blues, matte sand, beiges, and milky shades.
• High ceilings, Ideally, the ceilings are decorated with massive wooden beams. [17]
• Unsophisticated spontaneous, but functional décor.
• Mosaic elements are usually used in the authentic Mediterranean style.
• The walls are tiled or finished with stone or rough stucco with ceramic flooring tiles.
• Wooden pieces of furniture combined with wrought iron pieces.

more content

listen to:
koop island blues
Koop, Ane Brun

get in the mood

• How to adopt the Mediterranean decor and style
• Watch Inside Shay Mitchell's Mediterranean-Inspired Home by Architectural Digest

keywords

Tips to get inspired by the Mediterranean style:
• Add wrought iron and wooden furniture pieces to your design.
• Use largely scaled pieces of furniture.
• Keep handmade pieces that are well-used and loved in the Mediterranean spaces.
• Apply azujelos wall-tiles or stone finishes on the walls as well as textured stucco which is key in the style.
• Highlight or add wooden beams on your ceiling.
• Utilize wrought iron as your main metallic accent.
• Keep your color scheme warm and European-scenery-inspired. Aqua blues and earthy tones flavored with blush tones and muted green shades.
• Use arches as an opening to spaces and wall treatments.

Comfortable
Luxurious but Raw
Spontaneous
Nature-Inspired
Artsy

where to shop:

To find some Mediterranean style pieces, visit:
https://www.overstock.com/
https://www.luxedecor.com/
https://interiorsonline.com.au/

Etsy shops:
YWStudioCrafts
lePetitMorocco
StudioR12

wooden beams for ceilings

textured stucco for walls

arches are a big part of the style

77

mediterranean

materials & mood board

swatch

linens

swatch

rattan

stone

olive wood

wrought iron

terracotta

lookbook

N.C.S.

NCS S 1005-Y80R   NCS S 3050-Y80R

NCS S 0907-B20G   NCS S 1005-R80B

NCS S 3020-Y80R   NCS S 6020-R80B

style compatible *paint colors*

NESTING TABLES
Lexington Monterey Sands
Sandy Brown Cambria
Nesting Table
luxedecor.com

CHEST
Baxton Studio
Chest, White/Blue
Baxton Studio

LIGHTING
Feiss Allier
Weathered Oak
Wood & Antique
Forged Iron
luxedecor.com

CHAIR
DELPHI Dining
Chair
luxedecor.com

SOFA
Comfort Roll Arm
Slipcovered Sofa
Pottery Barn

COFFEE TABLE
Rockvale Stone
Top Round
Coffee Table by
Greyson Living
overstock.com

SPACE FOR creativity

Simple
Highly Functional
Sleek Lines
Uncluttered
Bold

Mid-Century Modern

MID-CENTURY MODERN

scan me with
your camera
to for more style inspo

scan me with
your camera
to get into the groove

swatch

Mid-Century Modern is gaining popularity for its **timeless** simplicity and high-quality craftsmanship. Utilizing natural finishes paired beautifully with handmade materials, **streamlined** pieces, and bolder color scheme that contrasts the simplicity of the components makes it a desirable style for the many.

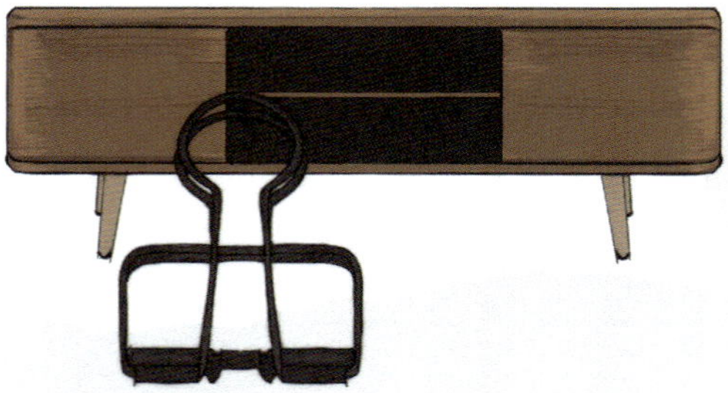

characteristics

- Functional forms that follow function.
- Tapered legs and "floating" furniture. [18]
- A balanced combination of synthetic and natural materials.
- Usage of bold colors, daring to use a complementary color scheme.
- Starbursts, atomic, and boomerang designs.
- The juxtaposition of different, sometimes contrasting, materials. [19]
- Streamline simplicity. Uncluttered and sleek lines with both organic and geometric forms.
- A visual interest created in geometrical prints and bold colors.

fun facts

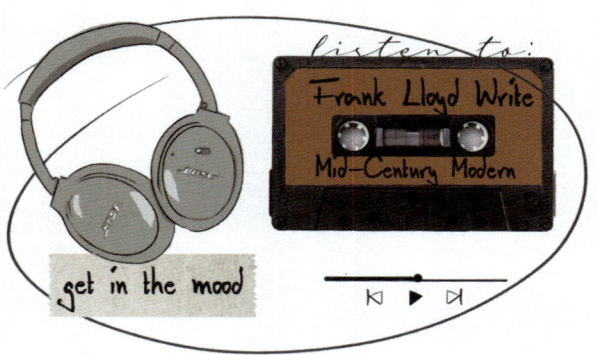

listen to:
Frank Lloyd Write
Mid-Century Modern

get in the mood

- Architectural Digest gave us a nice in-depth look into Mandy Moore's Mid-Century Modern house, which is so beautiful. To watch it by scanning the QR code!

- Harvey Specter's apartment in the T.V. show "Suits" is designed to be ultra modern with hints of mid-cenutry modern.

Tips to apply the Mid-Century Modern style to your interior:

• Simplify and remember less is more, the simpler the lines the better.
• Use tapered, higher legs furniture.
• Consider mixing natural materials with industrial hand-crafted metals.
• High-quality finishes are the key ingredient for a successful application of the style.
• The form is all about function in this style. Pick highly functional pieces.
• Get inspired by the beauty of geometrical shapes.
• Do not be afraid to experiment with bold color combinations especially retro-inspired colors. But you can make the style more contemporary by keeping the palette neutral.

Simple
Highly Functional
Sleek Lines
Uncluttered
Bold

where to shop:
To find some Mid-Century Modern style pieces, visit:
https://www.article.com/
https://www.westelm.com/
https://www.allmodern.com/
https://www.jet.com/
https://www.worldmarket.com/

Etsy shops:
MCModernStudio2
WoodArchitecture
AndersBrowneInterior
stoelenmeisje
commonorder

by:
Josh Hemsley

simplicity in wall treatments

heavy use of wooden accents

tapered legs,
"floating furniture"

mid-century modern

materials & *mood board*

swatch

leather

timber

brass

plastic

lookbook

N.C.S.

NCS S 0300-N	NCS S 3040-Y50R
NCS S 7010-Y30R	NCS S 2010-B90G
NCS S 3020-B40G	NCS S 3502-Y

style compatible *paint colors*

COFFEE TABLE
Whisler Coffee Table
ALLMODERN.COM

CUSHION
Arsdale Geometric
Cotton Throw
Pillow Cover
ALLMODERN.COM

LOVESEAT
Marcus Loveseat
ALLMODERN.COM

LIGHTING
Curvilinear
Mid-Century
Chandelier
West Elm

ARMCHAIR
Eames® Lounge Chair and
Ottoman

DESK
Culla Walnut Desk
article.com

SPACE FOR creativity

Simple
Clean lines
Uncluttered
High-Quality
Finished

Minimal

MINIMAL

scan me with
your camera
to for more style inspo

scan me with
your camera
to get into the groove

minimal

swatch

Minimalism is a lifestyle and philosophy that has been gaining a lot of exposure lately; because it enables the average person to experience life is a newly-profound light to value what's important. That's how the Minimal style also gained popularity. As it sheds light on **simplicity** in both form and function, devoiding the space of excessive decoration while creating **uncomplicated** open plans that focus on the day-to-day activity.

characteristics

- Less is more, uncluttered, but a finished space.
- Lots of open space paired with pristine, clean lines.
- Keeping only items of function.
- Massive windows to let in a lot of light.
- Monochromatic color scheme, with an accent of color, if any.
- High gloss surfaces.
- Luxurious and lush materials and finishes.
- Often associated with Modern style, but doesn't necessarily have to be modern.
- Celebration of the negative space.
- Keeping the essentials and valued items only.
- High-quality pieces, attention to detail. [21]

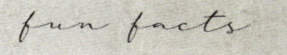

fun facts

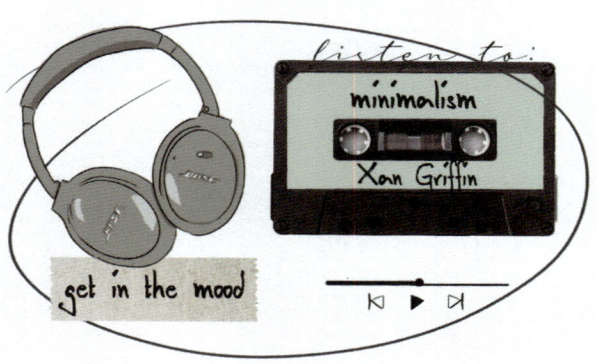

listen to:
minimalism
Xan Griffin

get in the mood

• The Minimalism movement was called many terms that including "A.B.C. Art", "Reductive Art", "Literalism", "Systematic Painting" and "Art of the Real". It was the term "Minimalism" that eventually kept its place, with the way it perfectly described the artists' minimal use of colors, shapes, lines and textures. [20]
Watch this family-friendly Minimalist Home by Designer Jeanette Hlinka

Get inspired by the minimal style by following those tips:

• Design your layout as open space. Less division and more negative space ensure better flow and circulation.

• Plan an asymmetrical layout to contrast the simplistic character of the space. Keep only functional pieces in the room.

• Utilize hidden storage as space needs to remain uncluttered.

• Choose furniture with solid colors and minimal designs.

• Keep a monochromatic color scheme.

• Enhance the natural light by keeping windows untreated, and surfaces high-shine.

• Invest in high-quality furniture, finishes, furnishings, and equipment, paying attention to detail.

• Create visual interest by having an abstract artwork, or exaggerated décor piece that contrasts the simplicity in the visual elements.

Simple
Clean lines
Uncluttered
High-Quality
Finished

where to shop:
To find some minimal style pieces, visit:
https://www.maisonsdumonde.com/
https://www.1stdibs.com/
https://www.finnishdesignshop.com/
https://www.onekingslane.com/
https://www.westelm.com/

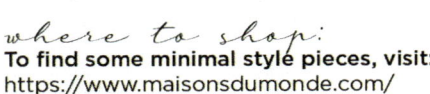

solid simple colors

clean lines,
high shine surfaces

minimal

materials & mood board

swatch

linen

marble

lookbook

N.C.S.

NCS S 0300-N	NCS S 1000-N
NCS S 2500-N	NCS S 5000-N
NCS S 7000-N	NCS S 8500-N

style compatible paint colors

LIGHTING
Flowerpot VP1
pendant, beige red
finnishdesignshop.com

COFFEE TABLE
Streamline Square
Coffee Table
westelm.com

FLOOR LAMP
Hudson Steel Shade
Floor Lamp
westelm.com

SIDE TABLE:
HIDEAWAY SIDE
TABLE WITH
STORAGE
CB2.com

DAYBED
Bon daybed Taigal 001
Master 80
finnishdesignshop.com

SOFA
Cloud LN2 sofa, 2-seater,
Sunniva 2/242
finnishdesignshop.com

Creativity

Clean
Tailored
Urban
Uncluttered
Casual

Modern

MODERN

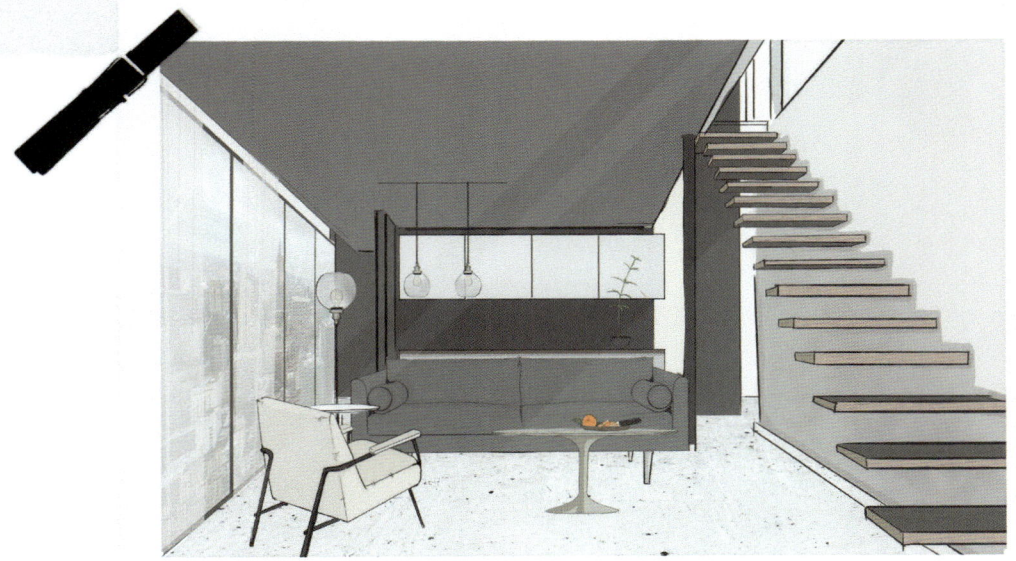

scan me with
your camera
to for more style inspo

scan me with
your camera
to get into the groove

modern

While modern and contemporary is often confused to be the same style, the modern style was actually started during the design movement of the 20th century, while contemporary style is about what's currently popular and is not tied to a historic era. [22]

The Modern style is pristine, sleek and industrial at the same time. Spaces are inviting, expansive and filled with light. The Modern style furnishings and decor celebrate natural materials eliminating unnecessary detailing. While you may see a range of colors in contemporary styling, modern styles would have monochromatic colors. [23]

characteristics

- Simple, solid lines.
- Minimal décor, unadorned spaces.
- Lower furniture with exposed legs.
- Geometric shapes.
- Polished shiny surfaces.
- Open spaces, untreated windows, with lots of natural light.
- Mostly neutral, monochromatic color scheme.
- Exposed structural elements.
- Natural materials in its raw form like wood, metals, leathers, and natural fibers.

fun facts

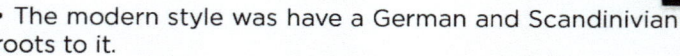

- The modern style was have a German and Scandinivian roots to it.

- Watch inside a $32 Million Upside Down House with Architectural Digest.

listen to:

fly me to the moon
Frank Sinatra

get in the mood

Tips to apply the modern style to your interior:
• Refrain from using curvy lines in the design instead of that opt for solid lines whether it's either vertical or horizontal.
• Only use a practical and functional home décor and accessories as form follows function strongly in the Modern style. Lack of décor is an important indication.
• Use polished reflective surfaces for your furniture pieces. Do not be afraid of using glass, especially when it comes to tabletops and countertops.
• Leave structural elements exposed such as concrete and beams. [23]
• Design a more open layout with bigger windows often with no treatment. Natural light is a big factor in modern interiors.
• Keep your color palette neutral and monochrome.
• Do not be afraid of using natural materials in their raw forms like wood, metals, leathers, and natural fibers.
• Add lower pieces of furniture with exposed legs.

Clean
Tailored
Urban
Uncluttered
Casual

where to shop:
To find some Mid-Century Modern style pieces, visit:
https://www.westelm.com/
https://www.allmodern.com/
https://www.ikea.com/
https://www.cb2.com/
https://www.crateandbarrel.com/

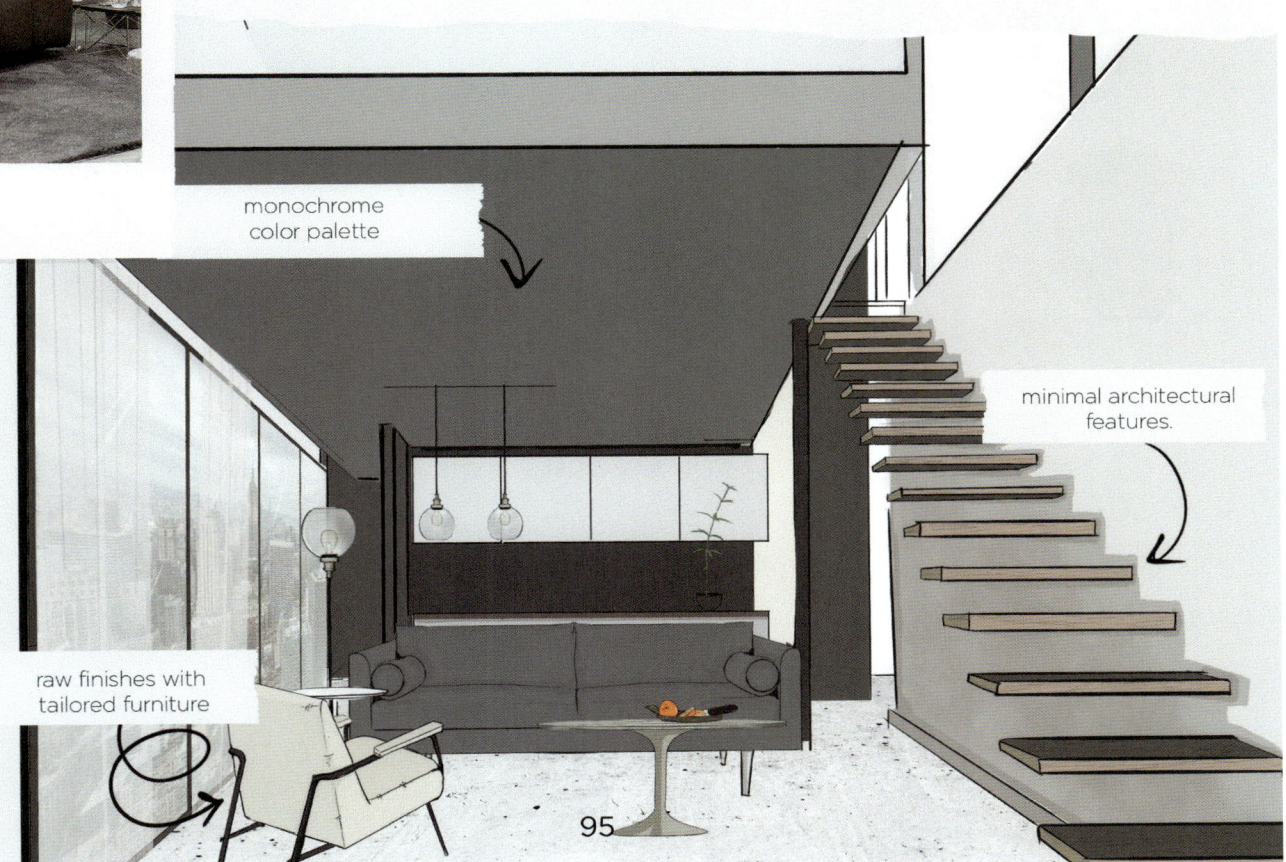

monochrome
color palette

minimal architectural
features.

raw finishes with
tailored furniture

modern

materials & mood board

swatch

leather

natural fibers

walnut wood

steel

look book

N.C.S.

style compatible *paint colors*

NCS S 0300-N

NCS S 3000-N

NCS S 1505-Y70R

NCS S 6005-Y80R

NCS S 8000-N

NCS S 3005-Y80R

COFFEE TABLE
Gibson Smoke Glass
Bunching Table
Crate and Barrel

FLOOR LAMP
RAW MARBLE
FLOOR LAMP
cb2.com

LIGHTING
Curvilinear
Mid-Century
Chandelier
WestElm.com

SOFA
Harmony Sofa
West Elm

BENCH
BESTÅ
TV bench with doors
IKEA.com

CHAIR
Nomad Leather
Safari Chair
cb2.com

Layered
Vivid
Colorful & Warm
Lush
Ornamented

Moroccan

MOROCCAN

scan me with
your camera
to for more style inspo

scan me with
your camera
to get into the groove

moroccan

swatch

This style was affected by several countries such as the Arab and Islamic cultures, Spain, France, and Portugal. The unique blending of Berber and Islamic styles create a very distinguished style. Some of the readily recognized features include geometric patterns, vivid colors, and zillij tiles. Zillij tiles are terra cotta tile-work of enamel chips set in plaster to create mosaic geometric shapes. [24]

Currently, the Moroccan style is used to bring in luxury and a multi-dimensional layer look to the interiors, it shows status and character. Being incredibly vivid and rich in ornaments made it a go-to look when it comes to people searching for a warmer and lush feel to their spaces.

julie aagnaard
@Julie.aagnaard

characteristics

- Vivid, lush, and layered.
- Colorful, warm, and inviting.
- Rough textures, heavily ornamented tiles play a big role in the style.
- Luxurious fabrics such as woven silk and Asian wool
- Adorned with décor, accessories, and ornaments.
- Arches are a part of the architectural elements of the style and they influence the space majorly (especially cinquefoil and multifoil arches).
- Water features, plants, and outdoor elements are brought in with a layered look to them.

fun facts

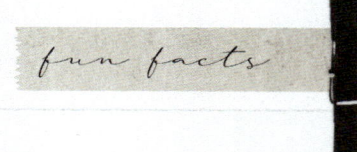

- The movie Aladdin Set design was inspired by the rich architectural details of Morocco.

- Watch Dar Shariq | Private Moroccan Riad by The Luxe Insider

listen to:

casablanca

Saad Lamjarred

get in the mood

⏮ ▶ ⏭

Tips to get inspired by the Moroccan style:

• Start with a strong architectural foundation. Use the columns and arches in the interior to your advantage.

• Use patterned ceramics and mosaic tiles to frame doors and windows. tabletops, and on accent pieces such as mirrors, picture frames, and wall art. [24]

• Layer your textures. A rough stucco finish to the wall against silk tapestry gives you the ultimate rich contrast woven silk rugs with ornaments are also used to infuse the space with comfort and luxury.

• Drape the room with textiles that are rich in color and texture, layer again with the lush Moroccan patterns

• Use carved wooden frames for furniture and overly-stuffed upholstered pieces.

• Rugged carved wood chests and tables are common. An inlay is typically bone, while other furniture lays are often Mother of Pearl designs. Contrast is the goal here.

• Upholster furniture includes reclining couches that are usually draped with fabric and accented with colorful pillows.

• Use over-stuffed ottomans are frequently as an accompaniment to chairs and sofas. [24]

keywords

Layered
Vivid
Colorful & Warm
Lush
Ornamented

where to shop:

To find some Moroccan style pieces, visit:
https://www.justmorocco.com/
https://theancienthome.com/
https://www.moroccanbazaar.com/
https://www.moroccanfurniturebazaar.com/
https://www.berbertrading.com/
https://www.casablancamarket.com/

Etsy Shops:
BerberMoroccanRugs
MoroccanWorldShop
LittleLightBazaar
BerberArtisanatFine
SquareMoroccan
EkenozMoroccanDecor

lush layered decor

pointed arches adorned with ornaments

over-stuffed ottomans

materials &
mood board

swatch

sabra silk

natural fibers

carved wood

bronze

N.C.S.

style compatible *paint colors*

NCS S 1010-Y60R	NCS S 7020-Y90R
NCS S 1010-B10G	NCS S 1005-B50G
NCS S 4050-Y90R	NCS S 2020-Y70R

lookbook

TABLE
MARSIE Bone Inlay Table
moroccanbazaar.com

RUG
Cordoba Rug
westelm.com

CUSHION
Jorja Cotton
Pillow Cover
wisteria.com

CHEST
Small Moroccan Inlaid Chest
TheParsonsPleasures on
Etsy.com

LIGHTING
Bronze Oxidize Brass
Pendant
EkenozMoroccanDecor
on Etsy.com

POUF
Embroidered Leather
Pouf, Chestnut
casablancamarket.com

SPACE FOR creativity

Respectful of History
Luxurious
Effortless
Embellished,
Lifestyle-Oriented

Parisian

scan me with
your camera
to for more style inspo

scan me with
your camera
to get into the groove

swatch

The Parisian style is heavily influenced by the Parisian chic lifestyle. It's an effortless luxury, highly dependent on embellished functionality and practicality. Respectful of the French crown molding and architectural context, reserving history while bringing on the modern touch, for the most part, it's a neutral space that has metallic touches and bold accent colors.

characteristics

- A contrast between more classical architectural details, like the French crown molding, and a more contemporary furniture style.
- Luxurious and lush, but effortless
- Sleek and practical, practical luxury.
- Embellished with brass and gold metallic accents.
- Mixing between the old and the new.
- Respecting the architectural context.
- Bold accents of colors.

fun facts

listen to:

la vie en rose

Édith Piaf

get in the mood

- Interior Design: How To Add Parisian Flair To Your Home by designer Ines Mazzotta of Kelly Hopter.
- Tour A Parisian-Inspired Family Home by designer Colette Varghese

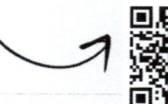

Get inspired by the Parisian style!
• Respect the architectural context, or mimic the Parisian architectural context if you crave that visual taste by having French crown moldings and wall moldings, as well as a ceiling medallion.
• Paint the crown molding in the same shade as the walls to create a simpler an effortless look to the interior.
• Practicality comes first in space planning, consider the lifestyle and adapt accordingly.
• Embellish interiors with brass and golden metallic touches.
• Mix the vintage and the contemporary.

Respectful of History
Luxurious
Effortless
Embellished,
Lifestyle-Oriented

where to shop:
To find some Parisian style pieces, visit:
https://www.maisonsdumonde.com/
https://www.1stdibs.com/
https://www.onekingslane.com/
https://www.westelm.com/
https://www.boconcept.com/

Etsy shops:
JustFrenchVintage
NEWANTIQUEfrench
MarieRicci
LuxeArchitectural
frenchvintagecloud

Allie Smith
@alliecoffeeandpassport

french crown molding and ceiling medallion

gilded mirror

contemporary furniture pieces

parisian

materials & *mood board*

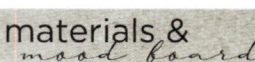

swatch — *velvet*

swatch — *cotton*

marble

brass

N.C.S.

NCS S 0300-N	NCS S 1005-Y
NCS S 1505-Y20R	NCS S 7010-G50Y
NCS S 1000-N	NCS S 3502-Y

style **compatible** *paint colors*

lookbook

COFFEE TABLE
Stanley Coffee Table, Smoked
Rippled Glass and Brass
Made.com

SOFA
Scott Large 2 Seater
Made.com

ACCENT ARMCHAIR
Moby
Accent Armchair
Made.com

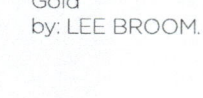

LIGHTING
Eclipse Chandelier
Gold
by: LEE BROOM.

MIRROR
19th Century
Louis-Philippe
Gilded Mirror

108

Rough
Untreated
Distressed
Coarse
Natural

Rustic

RUSTIC

scan me with
your camera
to for more style inspo

scan me with
your camera
to get into the groove

swatch

The Rustic style is all about raw materials, coarse finishes, and rich textures. The style is comfortable and homey, it feels lived in. It's very unsophisticated and rough. Furniture is scaled large and accessories are antique, think about a cabin in the woods when using the Rustic style as your main inspiration.

characteristics

- Coarse, rough and natural materials.
- Heavy use of untreated woods and stone.
- Vaulted wood ceilings.
- Unsophisticated, stable, and homey.
- Neutral and natural color palette.
- Distressed furniture that feels antique.
- Woven textiles and textured finishes.
- Completely stripped out of modern materials, like metals and plastics. Unless it is mixed with other styles (like contemporary). [25]

fun facts

listen to:

coffee

Sylvan Esso

get in the mood

• The rustic style is natural, warm and inviting. Modern finishes should be completely out of the picture. Natural materials are the only materials in the pure rustic style.
• Inside Aaron Paul's Rustic Riverside Home In Idaho, one of the best Rustic home tours ever.

Get inspired by the rustic style:
• Keep the architectural context rough and cottagey. Use natural materials such as reclaimed woods and stone.
• Use distressed wood to add a lived-in feel to the area.
• Maintain a cozy vibe by adding woven textiles in the main furniture pieces and furnishings.
• Layer and add depth by varying the sizes of the furniture and accessories.
• Thrift antique items that feel unique to accessorize the interior.
• Avoid using synthetic materials, or any shiny, geometrical or too polished elements. Unless you intend to mix it with another style.
• Keep a natural color scheme, deep tones are go-to in the Rustic style.

Rough
Untreated
Distressed
Coarse
Natural

where to shop:
To find some minimal style pieces, visit:
https://www.rusticfurniture.com/
https://woodlandcreekfurniture.com/
https://www.jossandmain.com/
https://www.blackforestdecor.com/
https://saltriverrustic.com/

Etsy Shops:
AllThatsRustic
AllAboutImpressions
RusticWoodHandcraft
OtherFurniture
SouthTexasHomeDecor

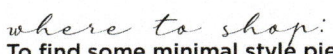

natural stone

deep warm tones

thrifted antique items

materials & *mood board*

swatch

animal skin

rustic woods

lookbook

N.C.S.

NCS S 6020-Y70R	NCS S 6030-Y70R
NCS S 4040-Y70R	NCS S 6020-Y20R
NCS S 7020-Y20R	NCS S 8500-N

style **compatible** *paint colors*

COFFEE TABLE
Otho Tufted Cocktail Ottoman
jossandmain.com

END TABLE
Dillon Spalted Primavera End Table
crateandbarrel.com

LIGHTING
Joon 6 - Light Candle Style Globe
jossandmain.com

CONSOLE:
Elvira 60" Console Table
Jossandmain.com

CHAIR
Lyster 29" W Armchair
jossandmain.com

SOFA
Bladen Loveseat
ashleyfurniture.com

Light
Sleek
Open
Minimal
Functional

Scandinavian

scan me with
your camera
to for more style inspo

scan me with
your camera
to get into the groove

scandinavian

intro

Simple spaces and well-made pieces, subdued colors, high contrasts, lots of wood, and botanical designs are what make the Scandinavian design beautiful. The simplicity and high quality of spaces, while it is on the minimalistic side of styles, it still achieves a cozy atmosphere. The use of warm tones and sepia hues and having white as a dominant color is a result of the weather in the Scandinavian countries being cloudy and dark for the most part, so brightening up spaces was a priority.

characteristics

- Clean, sleek, minimal lines, and a geometric touch.
- Timeless design pieces.
- A decluttered "less is more" approach, open plans are usually employed.
- Light blond wood such as birch, spruce, and pine.
- Muted and minimalistic color palettes, warm tones, and sepia hues.
- Big windows with sheer curtains.
- Minimal botanical designs and patterns.
- Hygge, which is a quality of coziness and comfortable conviviality that engenders a feeling of contentment or well-being (regarded as a defining characteristic of Danish culture).
- Multi-functional furniture pieces.

fun facts

- You can see the Scandinavian style in action in the movie: The Bridge
- Watch an HGTV designer's living room get a Scandi-style makeover

listen to:
familiar
Agnes Obel
get in the mood

118

Apply the Scandinavian style to your interior:
• Aim for an open layout.
•Less is more. Have a minimalistic approach in the space by using multifunctional pieces. A T.V. bench can double as a storage unit for example.
• Adapt a subdued color palette and make white your dominant color.
• Wooden floors and light wood furniture is a big factor of the style. Find pieces that are made from materials like birch, spruce or pine.
• Do not sacrifice the coziness of the space. Make it inviting by adding warm touches such as mood lights, throw blankets, and minimal yet aesthetically pleasing accessories.
• You can break the color palette with something brighter, like using a solid bright color in one of your furniture pieces, but do not go overboard with it.
• Keep only important pieces of accessories, this style does not tolerate clutter.

Light
Sleek
Open
Minimal
Functional

where to shop:
To find some Scandinavian style pieces, visit:
https://www.ikea.com/
https://www.finnishdesignshop.com/
https://bombinate.com/
https://www.jysk.com/
https://www.objekt.as/
https://fermliving.com/

subdued color palette

FIKA

light wood used mostly untreated (pine, birch, ash)

sheet window treatments to let more light in

1 7
AUGUST

scandinavian

materials & mood board

swatch

linen

natural fibers

light wood

N.C.S

NCS S 0603-Y60R NCS S 1505-Y60R

NCS S 2010-Y90R NCS S 2010-Y60R

NCS S 0500-N NCS S 0603-Y20R

style compatible *paint colors*

lookbook

COFFEE TABLE
LISABO
Coffee table
IKEA.com

LIGHTING
Capiz Rectangle
Chandelier
westelm.com

CHAIR
Muuto
Visu Lounge Chair
2modern.com

SOFA
NORSBORG
Finnsta white
IKEA.com

PAMPAS
Dried Plants Pampas
celestexmarketing
on: ebay.com

SIDEBOARD
Air sideboard, oak - cane
finnishdesignshop.com

120

creativity

Casual
Feminine
Distressed
Pastel
Hand-Made

Shabby Chic

SHABBY CHIC

scan me with
your camera
to for more style inspo

scan me with
your camera
to get into the groove

shabby chic

The shabby chic style takes the whole cottage style into a whimsical feminine atmosphere. While it might look cluttered if you are into more minimalistic styles, it has a lot more personality and character. It celebrates the diversity in patterns and textures. Currently, the style focuses on a pastel color scheme that is paired with distressed items that feel well-loved and adorned. Heavy in textile combinations and combining patterns.

Tania Miron

characteristics

• Often feminine collectibles as accessories, orderly staged clutter.
• Furniture and Accessories can be a little shabby, worn or a little weathered. But it's not dated nor ragged. [26] Hand-made feeling to the décor.
• Doors and mirrors and furniture pieces are often framed with faux crown moldings and distressed to liking.
• Soft and Pale color palette. Pastels are a notable key to this style.
• Florals, Plaids, and other patterns are used in a layered manner.
• Lace is a gorgeous décor element used heavily in window treatments as well as to slipcovers and table covers.
• Distressed furniture that feels antique. Chic in a "rumbled" way.
• Architectural elements are loved, in forms of moldings that are often distressed.
• Painted or rusted wrought iron for a shabby touch.

fun facts

• The restaurant, Shakespear&Co, adapted the shabby chic style as a part of its charm.
• "The Shabby chic style started in Great Britain back in the 1900s when country homeowners had financial struggles and wanted to deal with the situation that their furniture and furnishings aged over time (becoming shabby). This shabby home decor 'style' however became popular in the 1980s when the upper-middle classes began to add it into their interior designs by expressing it through their classically vintage furniture as a way of showing that they had class and taste. In addition, it took hints from the French-style". [27]

listen to:
lollipop
The Chordettes
get in the mood

Tips to get inspired by the Shabby Chic style:
• Use crown moldings and wall trims and give them a shabbier look by distressing them.
• Do not be afraid of mixing patterns like florals, stripes, and plaid.
• Apply a calm pastel color scheme to the design, pale minty green paired with a pastel shade of pink and lots of whites to balance it out.
• Slipcovered grand sofas and furniture pieces are usually the heart of a shabby chic interior.
• Layer fabrics with contrast in textures creatively using laces and textured fabrics.
• DIY's are very common; a hand-made infusion is often associated with the shabby chic style.
• Distress raw materials and rust metals like wrought iron. Use metals that are more matt and rustic.

keywords

Casual
Feminine
Distressed
Pastel
Hand-Made

where to shop:

To find some Shabby Chic style pieces, visit:
http://www.thepaintedcottagestudio.com/
http://www.cottagechicstore.com/
https://www.shabbychic.com/
https://www.kathykuohome.com/
https://www.belleescape.com/

Etsy Shops:
Upcycledfairies
mooshop
RoseCottageChic
ShabbyChicTables
SageandBalmInteriors

distressed furniture

feminine pieces

classical silhouette

shabby chic

materials & mood board

swatch

lace

swatch

natural fibers

PHOTO CREDIT: Sündenherz on Flickr
https://www.suendenherz.de/

white washed wood

N.C.S.

NCS S 1005-B80G

NCS S 1010-Y90R

NCS S 1010-R40B

NCS S 0505-Y40R

NCS S 3005-B80G

NCS S 0804-G90Y

style compatible *paint colors*

lookbook

ROSES
Bouquets   50 c

ARTWORK
Romantic Shabby Cottage Chic
Wood Sign By Debi Coules
DebiCoulesArt on Etsy.com

LIGHTING
Madeline White
Shabby Chic
Chandelier
belleescape.com

SOFA
Shabby Chic Dust
Ruffle Settee
belleescape.com

CHAISE
Eloquence Marie Antoinette Chaise in
Silver Antique White Tone
kathykuohome.com

TRUNK
Vintage Aqua Trunk
with Fabric Liner
shabbychic.com

Symmetrical
Predictable
Harmonious
Orderly
Familiar
Consistent

Traditional

TRADITIONAL

scan me with
your camera
to for more style inspo

scan me with
your camera
to get into the groove

traditional

swatch

intro

The inspiration for the Traditional style comes from the 18th and 19th-century interiors. It is homey, unfussy, and predictable. Older generations prefer this style as it's comfortable while being well-designed for functionality. Layouts are unsurprising and spaces are used for their assigned roles. Hardwoods and natural materials are heavily used in the style.

characteristics

- Predictable, familiar, harmonious, and orderly.
- Largely-scaled pieces of furniture.
- Furnishings are classic and might feel outdated. Unsurprising elements with matching and consistent pieces. [28]
- Sets of furniture that match are often used.
- Upholstered and sophisticated furniture pieces.
- Functional, modest, and restful looking. Edges are soft, smooth, and blended into the whole interior. [28]
- Nothing is too shiny or too harsh.
- Trims and crown moldings are often finished with glossy white paint.
- Symmetrical layouts.
- Darker shades of stained woods and stone are used in the context of floors, walls, and furniture.
- Window coverings in traditional rooms show a classic style. Look for narrow shutters, traverse draperies, and under treatments of pinch pleated sheers. Cornices and valances may also be featured. [28]

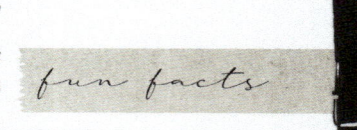

fun facts

listen to:

old school

Liimo

get in the mood

- You can see the Traditional style in action in the movies: Darkest Hour and the T.V. Show: Mad Men.
- In the movie 500 Days of Summer, Tom's parents' house followed the traditional style rule by rule.

Tips to get inspired by the traditional style:
• Utilize each room for its specific function. Living room for relaxing and hosting guests, dining room for eating. Functionality driven space planning is the main element of the style.
• Use a matching set of rigid furniture pieces with curves in the trims.
• Apply dark stained finishes to woods. Employ hardwood flooring and natural materials generously.
• Use darker warm tones as your main palette of colors. [29]
• Incorporate classical art and antiques to infuse the style with life.
• Regal influenced pieces of furniture are appropriate to exploit in the style.
• Grand accessories to be used like big vases, china, candle holders, and traditional chandeliers.

keywords

Symmetrical
Predictable
Harmonious
Orderly
Familiar
Consistent

where to shop:
Online shops for traditional pieces:
https://www.ashleyfurniture.com/
https://www.birchlane.com/
https://www.wayfair.com/
https://www.ffdm.com/
https://www.taylorsclassics.com/

Etsy shops:
HighEndUsedFurniture
ChatsworthAntiques

employment of a stone fireplace

symmetry

warm colors palette

traditional

materials & mood board

swatch

viscose

swatch

leather

zebra wood

silver

N.C.S.

NCS S 6030-R

NCS S 7010-Y70R

NCS S 1505-Y70R

NCS S 6020-R

NCS S 5030-Y30R

NCS S 1505-Y30R

style compatible paint colors

lookbook

DESK:
Tyler Creek 60"
Home Office Desk
ashleyfurniture.com

OFFICE CHAIR:
Fairfax Executive
Desk Chair
countrysideamishfurniture.com

SOFA:
Olsberg Sofa
ashleyfurniture.com

LIGHTING:
ÄPPELVIKEN
Chandelier
IKEA.com

ARMCHAIR:
STOCKSUND
Segersta multicolour
IKEA.com

SPACE FOR creativity

Contrasted
Blended
Sophisticated
Clean
Comfortable

Transitional

TRANSITIONAL

scan me with
your camera
to for more style inspo

scan me with
your camera
to get into the groove

swatch

The transitional style bridges traditional and contemporary design styles exclusively. It focuses on mixing masculine pieces with more feminine pieces, creating a sophisticated outcome. Dark wooden accents are paired with more streamlined-contemporary pieces.

characteristics

- Exclusively bridges traditional and contemporary styles.
- Embraces the lines of the traditional style while giving it a contemporary makeover with the colors and furnishings
- Neutral colors. It can include the tone-on-tone color scheme.
- Sophisticated and luxurious feel to the interior.
- Clean lines that often lack ornaments and clutter.
- A contrast in textures and different materials, such as suede, chenille, and leather. [30]
- Comfortable and functional natural materials are blended with more contemporary materials like stainless steel and glass.

fun facts

- What's great about the style is that it balances masculine and feminine attributes, it focuses on the best qualities of the contemporary style and traditional style, taking functionality as an anchor.

Watch Transitional home for todays modern family by Robeson Design - Kinwoven

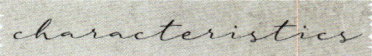
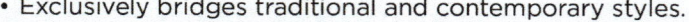

listen to:
viva la vida
Coldplay

get in the mood

Tips to get inspired by the Transitional style:
• Juxtapose the existing architectural context. If it is more traditional with trims and moldings, then choose sleeker lines furniture pieces for a contemporary touch and vise versa.
• Use a neutral color palette. Tone-on-tone can work pretty well too.
• Scale your accessories to be in a similar size, an accent piece can be added when needed.
• Add glass and metallic touches to embellish your interior.
• Find furniture pieces that contain visible darker wooden frames.
• Pick sloped arm sofas and accent chairs.

Contrasted
Blended
Sophisticated
Clean
Comfortable

where to shop:
To find some transitional style pieces, visit:
https://www.cb2.com/
https://www.crateandbarrel.com/
https://www.zarahome.com/
https://www.indigo-living.com/
https://www.westelm.com/
https://www.2xlme.com/

feminine details
mixed with masculine lines

contemporary
furniture

tufted pieces mixed
with wooden accents

transitional

materials & mood board

swatch

linen

dark wood

golden accents

lookbook

ARMCHAIR
Hallie 21" Armchair
by House of Hampton
on: wayfair.ca

N.C.S.

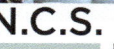

NCS S 2010-B50G	NCS S 7010-Y50R
NCS S 1010-B10G	NCS S 1005-B50G
NCS S 0500-N	NCS S 8005-B20G

style compatible *paint colors*

LIGHTING
Capiz Rectangle
Chandelier
westelm.com

TABLE
Sagamore X-Leg Ottoman
by Rosdorf Park
on: wayfair.com

SOFA
Paidge Sofa
westelm.com

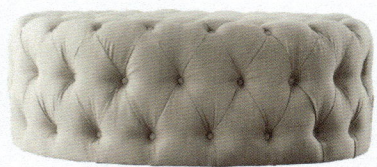

OTTOMAN
Bourges Cocktail Ottoman
by Feminine French Country
on: wayfair.com

COFFEE TABLE
BERET MARBLE 2-TIER
COFFEE TABLE
CB2.com

creativity

Layered
Authentic
Earthy
Rich
Textured

Tribal

TRIBAL

scan me with
your camera
to for more style inspo

scan me with
your camera
to get into the groove

tribal

swatch

The African Tribal is a delicious style that feels like a wild safari trip in the middle of Africa. It's rich in colors, patterns, materials, and textures. It has an eclectic undertone to it which makes it a great style to mix. Woven furniture frames combined with layered furnishings and dark shades of espresso-colored woods are a typical quality of the Tribal style that induces seasoned coziness.

characteristics

- Authentic and rich.
- Geometric tribal patterns such as Kuba print.
- Earthy and rich dark shades of colors.
- Dark rustic shades of wood.
- Layered look with eclectic pieces.
- Mergeable with different styles.
- Textured walls, plaster, and wallpaper.
- Woven pieces of furniture, baskets, and accessories.
- Natural materials like rattan combined with leathers.
- African pottery and accessories.
- Inspired by the wild animal prints and animal skins.

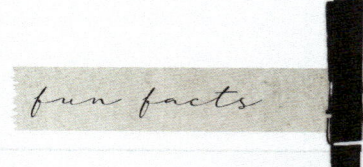

fun facts

- Production Designer Hannah Beachler won Best Production Design at the 91st Academy Awardsin Hollywood for her work on Marvel's Black Panther which features the African Tribal style in multiple scenes.
- The fascination for Africa and South or Central America are the inspiration for the Ethnic furniture style.

listen to:

vibrations

Fireboy DML

get in the mood

142

Tips to get inspired by the tribal style:
• Maintain a natural look to the finishes that are inspired by clay houses. Keep the plaster textured and rough. You can also use wallpaper to add depth and texture.
• Opt for woven pieces of furniture as main or accent pieces.
• Stain wood in a dark-espresso shade or use carved wooden pieces.
• Layer furnishings. Mix and match wild patterns with geometric patterns noting that ethnic-inspired patterns work well with this style.
• Decorate with rustic and raw pottery.
• Use materials like rattan, jute, suedes, animal skins, and leathers to infuse nature into space.

Layered
Authentic
Earthy
Rich
Textured

where to shop:

To find some tribal style pieces, visit:
https://houseofavana.com/
https://www.crateandbarrel.com/
https://discoverafricanart.com/
https://www.africancraftsmarket.com/
https://www.novica.com/

Etsy Shops:
RoyalStencils
Houseofjujuhats
comptoirdesfactories
OldWoodenStool
IBABARugs

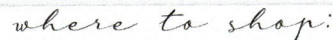

raw finishes

woven pieces,

mix of ethnic patterns

143

tribal

materials & mood board

swatch

leather

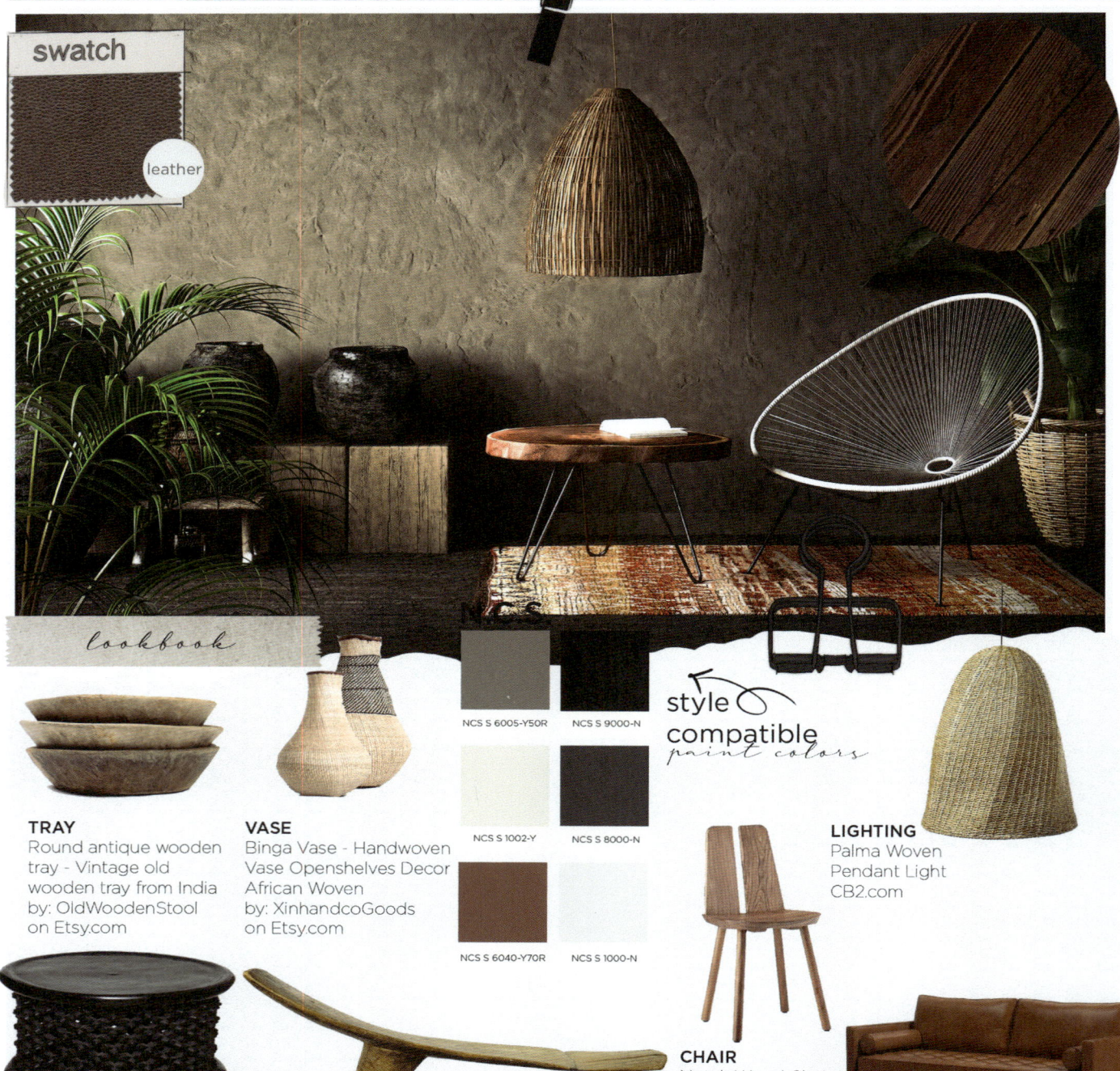

lookbook

style compatible *paint colors*

NCS S 6005-Y50R	NCS S 9000-N
NCS S 1002-Y	NCS S 8000-N
NCS S 6040-Y70R	NCS S 1000-N

TRAY
Round antique wooden
tray - Vintage old
wooden tray from India
by: OldWoodenStool
on Etsy.com

VASE
Binga Vase - Handwoven
Vase Openshelves Decor
African Woven
by: XinhandcoGoods
on Etsy.com

LIGHTING
Palma Woven
Pendant Light
CB2.com

CHAIR
Notch Wood Chair
CB2.com

COFFEE TABLE
First class African hand carved
Bamileke
by Houseofjujuhats
on Etsy.com

CHAIR
Senufo Three Legged
Chair– Ivory Coast
discoverafricanart.com

SOFA
Monroe Mid-Century
Tufted Seat Leather Sofa
westelm.com

SPACEFOR *Creativity*

Laid-Back
Fresh
Quirky
Eclectic
Colorful, and Airy

Tropical

TROPICAL

scan me with
your camera
to for more style inspo

scan me with
your camera
to get into the groove

tropical

swatch

When you see a design of a Tropical style room, it immediately transcends you to a **vacation** state of mind. With statement pieces of furniture, an eclectic touch of course, and fun quirky prints, with a tremendous amount of leafy greeneries and plants, this style is **dynamic** and **fresh**.

characteristics

- A laid-back and relaxed style.
- Wicker furniture.
- Inspired by the islands and beaches of Hawaii.
- Sisal, jute, wicker, and seagrass used as materials.
- Mixed graphic prints.
- Wooden carved furniture.
- A quirky mix of patterns and eclectic pieces of furniture.
- Using big leafy plants like banana leaf.

fun facts

- Eat, Pray, Love movie starring Julia Roberts portrays a neutral Tropical interior in her Bali Hut.
- Another more contemporary take on the Tropical style is in the T.V. Show: Jane The Virgin, where the hotel most of the scenes take place: The Marbella follows a glam take on the Tropical style.

listen to:

we dont talk anymore

DJ Tich — Tropical Mix

get in the mood

keywords

Laid-Back
Fresh
Quirky
Eclectic
Colorful, and Airy

Tips to apply the Tropical Style:
• Use lighter and brighter hues of colors. Think about the colors of a beach alongside nature when picking out a fresh color scheme.
• Infuse the space with lush leafy greenery to bring the outside in.
• Apply natural seagrass and wicker throughout the room.
• Infuse the style with some coastal, even nautical touches, and add elements like hammocks or tiki torches into the indoor (or outdoor) context.
• You can also steer the design into a more elegant tropical style by applying the tropical motifs as wallpapers and opting for simpler style furniture pieces.
• You can also opt for a rain-forest type of tropical design that includes more daring prints and patterns such as tropical flowers or birds.

where to shop:
shop pieces inspired by the tropical style:
https://www.finnishdesignshop.com/
http://tropicalfurnituregallerycc.com/
https://www.furniture.com/
https://www.wickerparadise.com/
https://www.ikea.com/

quirky tropical patterns + tropical plants

rattan as a main element

fresh color palette

17 AUGUST

CHANEL

tropical

materials & *mood board*

swatch

linens

swatch

sheers

wood

rattan

lookbook

N.C.S.

NCS S 5010-G30Y	NCS S 1510-G20Y
NCS S 7010-B90G	NCS S 0540-Y

style **compatible** *paint colors*

FAUX PLANT:
FEJKA
Artificial potted
plant, in/outdoor
Monstera
IKEA.com

LIGHTING:
Arwen Wicker
Pendant Light
CB2.com

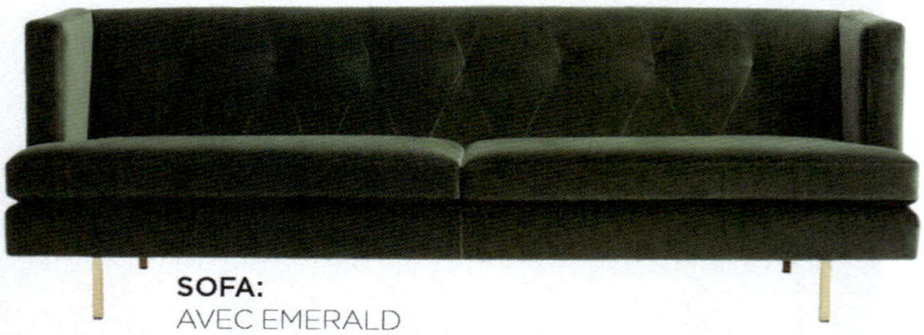

CHAIR:
BUSKBO
Armchair, rattan
IKEA.com

STOOL:
ALSEDA
Stool, banana fibre
IKEA.com

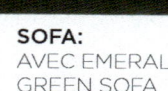

SOFA:
AVEC EMERALD
GREEN SOFA
CB2.com

SPACE FOR *Creativity*

mini-guide to:
mixing & matching
interior design styles:

1- Start with a concept then visualize it with a mood board: the concept will give you a **creative direction** and a general theme toexplore the styles. A mood board is a tool to gather these ideas and translate them into a **visual manifestation**. By putting together items that go with your concept into a mood board, you can eyeball how cohesive they look.

2- Functionality is everything: no matter how good the room looks, if it fails to serve the users, then it is doesn't work. When you **put functionality first**, it will help tremendously with choosing the right pieces. Think of the **layout** first and **study the circulation** of the room, then mixing the styles will be a lot easier when you know what goes where.

3- Maintain a limited color palette: this doesn't mean that everything should be monochromatic or neutral, although that is an option if this is the look you are going for. Choosing a specific color scheme will help tie the room together. It will create a more cohesive overall look. Repeat the same color throughout the space for a more unified look. [31]

4- Use the 60-30-10% rule: while most designers utilize this rule with creating color schemes *(as an example: 60% is the overall color, big pieces of furniture, and larger pieces like rugs, 30% is for smaller pieces, curtains, and accent chairs, and 10% is for the throw cushions and other smaller furnishings, vases, and accessories).* You can utilize this rule with the style mixing, keep 60% of the room to a specific foundation style, complement it with 30% of another style. Finally, add a small accent of a quirky style to add a playful touch to the room.

4- Match the woods[31] : one of the oldest tricks in the book, even if two pieces of furniture are from totally different styles, if they have the same wooden hue, then matching them will be massively easier. It doesn't mean you can't mix your woods, but it makes it smoother to do so. BONUS TIP: if you want to mix woods, pay attention to the grain color and find a middle ground.

5- Simpler pieces with accent pieces: there are sofas and other pieces of furniture that don't have a style. They are simple, streamline, and forgiving when you want a subtle mix of styles. If you keep the foundation relatively simple, you can afford to mix more styles in the room, creating a unique personality to the space.

6- There are no rules: remember that other humans are the ones who created the interior design styles as a mere suggestion to apply [31]. There are no set-in-stone rules. If you wish to explore and experiment with what you or your client wants, then by all means more power to you. With experience, you will learn that taking risks with interior styling results in spaces that are filled with personality.

7- Easier to mix styles: if you wish to learn what styles are easier to mix, look at the matrix in the next page, use it as a tool if you wish.

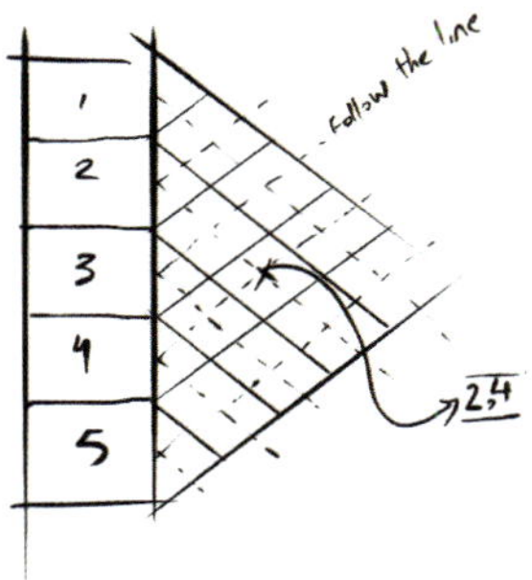

This matrix is a guide that helps you understand which styles are easier to mesh based on how many traits they have in common. Most styles are a complex blend of several different periods and ears. I am encouraging you to explore if you are curious despite what the matrix here indicates. But I hope this saves you some valuable time.

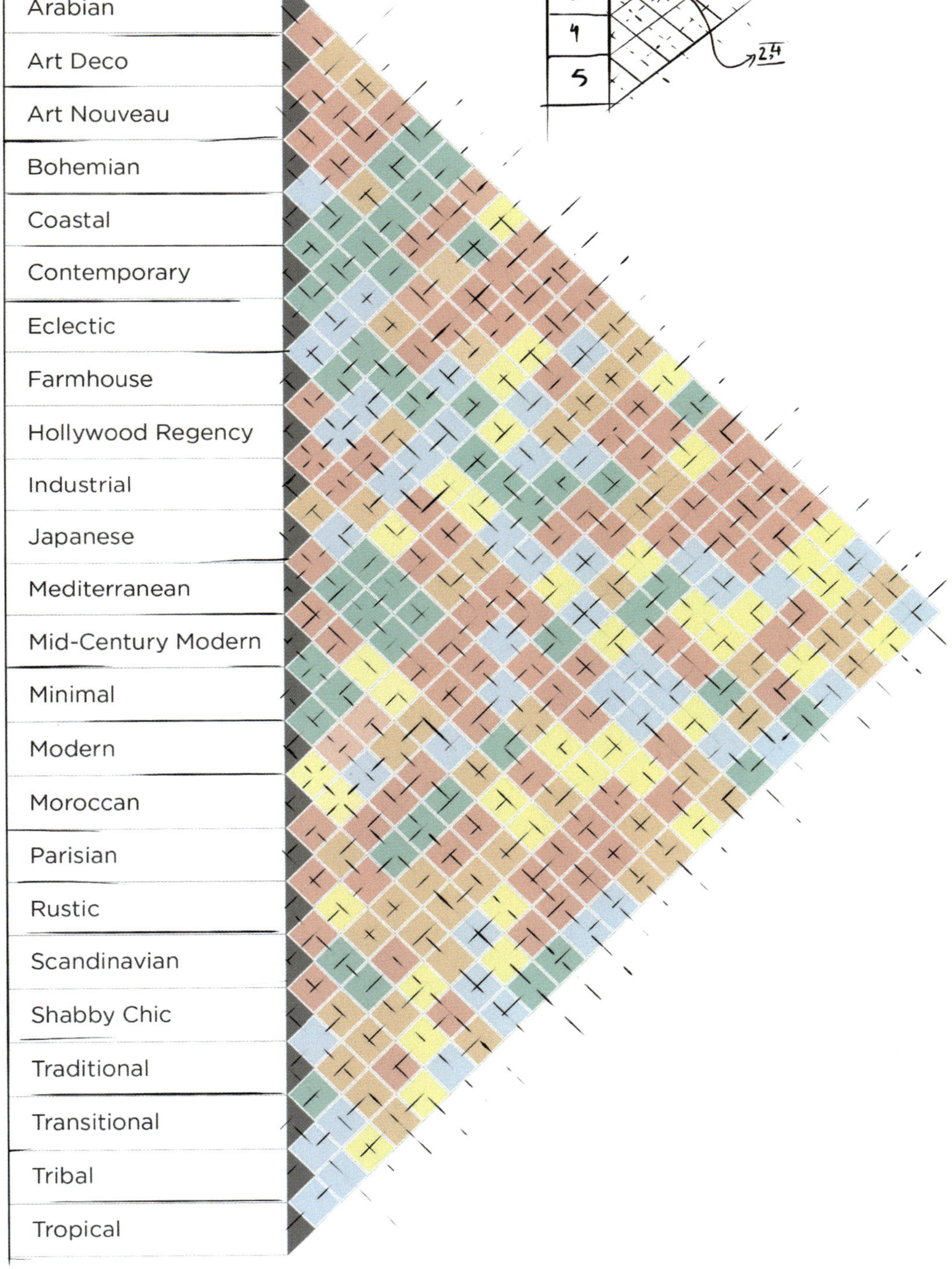

LEGEND

- Very Easy
- Easy
- Medium
- Hard
- Very Hard

Arabian

Art Deco

Art Nouveau

Bohemian

Coastal

Contemporary

Eclectic

Farmhouse

Hollywood Regency

Industrial

Japanese

Mediterranean

Mid-Century Modern

Minimal

Modern

Moroccan

Parisian

Rustic

Scandinavian

Shabby Chic

Traditional

Transitional

Tribal

Tropical

MORE TO *explore*

Here you will find a list of recommended resources to learn more about Interior Design styles and how they developed historically.`
You can also retrieve the list of resources and websites by visiting my website
https://www.aseelbysketchbook.com/resources

GET IT FROM **amazon**

SCAN THE CODE

The Guide to Period Styles for Interiors:
From the 17th Century to the Present
by **Judith Gura**

The Abrams Guide to Period Styles for Interiors
by **Judith Gura**

A History of Interior Design 3rd Edition
by **John F. Pile**

Judith Miller Guide to Period Style Curtains and
Soft Furnishings
by **Judith Miller**

Period Design and Furnishing
by **Martin Miller**

The Finer Things: Timeless Furniture,
Textiles, and Details
by **Christiane Lemieux**

MORE TO *explore*

**Websites to learn more about
Interior Design Styles
List is also available on
www.aseelbysketchbook/resources**

https://www.thespruce.com
https://decorinteriorsus.com
https://www.mydomaine.com
https://www.homedit.com
https://www.housebeautiful.com
https://www.decoraid.com
https://www.smalldesignideas.com
https://www.pufikhomes.com
https://filmandfurniture.com
https://www.homestratosphere.com
https://blog.froy.com
https://www.decorilla.com
https://www.craftside.net
https://www.hgtv.com
https://www.apartmenttherapy.com
https://freshome.com
https://mrkate.com
https://www.interiorfun.com
https://www.elledecor.com
https://www.aseelbysketchbook.com

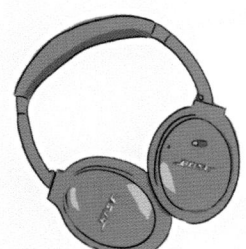

**brain food, music for
when you are browsing**

⏮ ▶ ⏭

BIBLIOGRAPHY

& resources

The Full List of Resources is Available on www.aseelbysketchbook.com/resources

1 Ernst J. Grube, J. D. (2011). *Architecture of the Islamic World* . London : Thames & Hudson .

2 Gura, J. (2005). The Abrams *Guide to Period Styles for Interiors* . New York : Harry N. Abrams Inc., Publishers.

3 Guides, T. A. (2017). *Art Deco Interior Design Guide*. Retrieved from The Art of Bespoke: https://www.theartofbespoke.com/editorial/art-deco

4 Gura, J. (2005). *The Abrams Guide to Period Styles for Interiors* . New York : Harry N. Abrams Inc., Publishers.

5 Gura, J. (2005). *The Abrams Guide to Period Styles for Interiors* . New York : Harry N. Abrams Inc., Publishers.

6 Smart, B. (2013, 11 12). *How to Achieve Bohemian (or "Boho-Chic") Style*. Retrieved from Homedit: https://www.homedit.com/how-to-achieve-bohemian-or-boho-chic-style/

7 LIVERMORE, S. (2018, 10 19). *Everything You Need To Know About Bohemian Design* Retrieved from: HouseBeautiful: https://www.housebeautiful.com/design-inspiration/a23748087/what-is-bohemian-design-style/

8 LIVERMORE, S. (2018, 10 19). *Everything You Need To Know About Bohemian Design.* Retrieved from HouseBeautiful: https://www.housebeautiful.com/design-inspiration/a23748087/what-is-bohemian-design-style/

9 LIVERMORE, S. (2018, 11 2). *Everything You Need To Know About Coastal Design.* Retrieved from HouseBeautiful: https://www.housebeautiful.com/design-inspiration/a24276474/coastal-design-style/

10 Nafie, C. (2019, 3 13). *How to Decorate in Contemporary Style.* Retrieved from TheSpruce : https://www.thespruce.com/designer-guide-to-contemporary-style-1976503

11 HGTV, *Contemporary Style 101.* (D.O.V. 2020). Retrieved from HGTV: https://www.hgtv.com/design/decorating/design-101/contemporary-style-101

12 NAVEED. (n.d.). *HOLLYWOOD REGENCY STYLE DEFINED AND HOW TO MAKE IT WORK FOR YOU.* Retrieved from decoraid: https://www.decoraid.com/blog/interior-design-style/hollywood-regency-style

13 NAVEED. (2019, 4 22). *INDUSTRIAL STYLE INTERIOR DESIGN: EVERYTHING YOU NEED TO KNOW.* Retrieved from decoraid.: https://www.decoraid.com/blog/interior-design-styles-definition/industrial-style

14 Flanagan, L. (2019, 8 18). *Industrial Chic Style.* Retrieved from TheSpruce: https://www.thespruce.com/industrial-chic-style-2213412

15 DYKH. (2020). *Interesting Facts about Japanese Houses.* Retrieved from Did You Know Home : https://didyouknowhomes.com/interesting-facts-about-japanese-houses/

16 Bartosch, K. S. (2019, 07 31). *Mediterranean Decorating Ideas for Bedrooms.* Retrieved from TheSpruce: https://www.thespruce.com/mediterranean-decorating-ideas-for-bedrooms-350650

17 Pufik, S. (2017, 6 24). *Mediterranean Style in Interior Design: romance of the south coast in your home.* Retrieved from Pufik Homes : https://www.pufikhomes.com/en/stili-interera/sredizemnomorskiy-stil/

18 VintageHomeBoutique (D.O.V. 2020). *Mid-Century Modern Furniture* Retrieved from VintageHomeBoutique : https://vintagehomeboutique.ca/pages/mid-century-modern-furniture

19 Abbas, A. (2019, 9 16) *5 Things You Should Know About the Mid-Century Modern Style.* Retrieved from TheSpruce: https://www.thespruce.com/things-you-should-know-about-mid-century-1391827

20 ArtListr, (2018 8 4) *Minimalism – 6 Interesting Facts.* Retrieved from ArtListr: https://artlistr.com/minimalism-6-interesting-facts/

21 Admin, S. S. (2018, 6 29). *Characteristics and Styles Of Minimalist Home Design.* Retrieved from sefastone: https://sefastone.com/blogs/s/minimalist-home-design

22 Toro, I. (2018, 10 29). *Characteristics of Modern Interior Design Style.* Retrieved from: Cowhide Outlet: https://cowhideoutlet.com/blog/characteristics-of-modern-interior-design-style/

23 Lee, T. (2019, 10 14). *Understanding the Modern Style of Décor.* Retrieved from: TheSpruce : https://www.thespruce.com/decorating-in-the-modern-style-452457

24 Painter, S. (2006-2020). Interior Design - Love to Know. Retrieved from Love To Know: https://interiordesign.lovetoknow.com/Moroccan_Interior_Design

25 LIVERMORE, S. (2018, 10 26). *Everything You Need to Know About Rustic Design.* Retrieved from: HouseBeautiful: https://www.housebeautiful.com/design-inspiration/a23937828/rustic-design-style/

26 Lee, T. (2019, 03 06). *Characteristics of Shabby Chic or Cottage-Style Decorating.* Retrieved from TheSpruce : https://www.thespruce.com/decorating-shabby-chic-or-cottage-style-452462

27 Turner, V. (2016, 11 2) *INTERESTING FACTS YOU SHOULD KNOW ABOUT SHABBY CHIC.* Retrieved from: TheAlmaMarket: https://www.thealmamarket.co.uk/blog/interesting-facts-you-should-know-about-shabby-chic

28 Nafie, C. (2019, 8 14). *Interior Decorating in the Traditional Style.* Retrieved from TheSpruce: https://www.thespruce.com/decorating-in-the-traditional-style-1977669

29 LIVERMORE, S. (2018, 10 12). *Everything You Need To Know About Traditional Design.* Retrieved from HouseBeautiful: https://www.housebeautiful.com/design-inspiration/a23611149/traditional-design/

30 Lee, T. (2019, 11 11). *The Perfect Transitional Decor.* Retrieved from TheSpruce: https://www.thespruce.com/decorating-in-the-transitional-style-452459

31 Lee, T. (2019, 8 19). Retrieved from: TheSpruce: https://www.thespruce.com/how-to-mix-decorating-styles-452089

meet the author

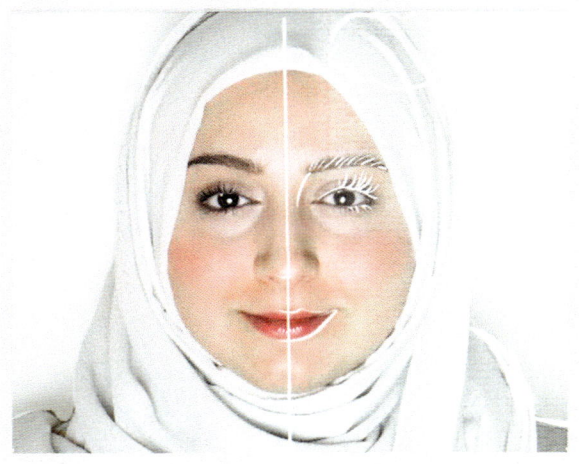

Aseel A. H.

Interior Designer, Illustrator, Content Creator & Entrepreneur.

Come & virtually hang out with me! :)
YOUTUBE: www.youtube.com/c/aseelbysketchbook
INSTAGRAM: www.instagram.com/aseelbysketchbook
WEBSITE: www.aseelbysketchbook.com
PINTEREST: www.pinterest.com/aseelbysketchbook
TWITTER: AbySketchbook

a final playlist for you,
thank you.

⏮ ▶ ⏭

All Rights Reserved © 2020 Aseel A. H. Ahmad
Aseel By Sketchbook
www.aseelbysketchbook.com

Printed in Poland
by Amazon Fulfillment
Poland Sp. z o.o., Wrocław

55800648R00093